MATH Trailblazers®

A BALANCED MATHEMATICS PROGRAM INTEGRATING SCIENCE AND LANGUAGE ARTS

Unit Resource Guide
Unit 10

Numbers and Patterns:
An Assessment Unit

THIRD EDITION

KENDALL/HUNT PUBLISHING COMPANY
4050 Westmark Drive   Dubuque, Iowa 52002

A TIMS® Curriculum
University of Illinois at Chicago

UIC The University of Illinois
at Chicago

The original edition was based on work supported by the National Science Foundation under grant
No. MDR 9050226 and the University of Illinois at Chicago. Any opinions, findings, and conclusions
or recommendations expressed in this publication are those of the author(s) and do not necessarily
reflect the views of the granting agencies.

Letter Home

Numbers and Patterns: An Assessment Unit

Date: _____

Dear Family Member:

In this unit your child will reflect on what he or she has done in math so far this year. Your child will help create a stencil border for the classroom and plan an imaginary class party. Your child will use many of the concepts we have been working on—the TIMS Laboratory Method, place value, addition, subtraction, multiplication, and division. The work will be assessed for understanding of math content, solving problems, and communicating solutions.

Your child will also take a midyear test to assess his or her knowledge of the concepts and skills covered in the first nine units and a separate test to gauge progress with the subtraction facts. Finally, as part of our ongoing reflection process, your child will spend time reviewing his or her portfolio. We will discuss work your child has done since the beginning of the year.

As we look back over what your child has learned in math, you can provide additional support at home by doing activities such as the following:

Child's drawing to show length of stenciled border

- Encourage your child to bring home any math games we played. Each game provides an excellent review.
- Ask your child to bring home his or her *Subtraction Facts I Know* chart. Work with your child to review the subtraction facts he or she finds difficult. Encourage your child to talk about different mental strategies he or she can use to recall those facts more quickly.

Thank you for your continued efforts to help your child with math ideas through discussion and games.

Sincerely,

_____

Carta al hogar

Números y patrones: Una unidad de evaluación

Fecha: _____

Estimado miembro de familia:

En esta unidad, su hijo/a reflexionará acerca de lo que ha hecho en la clase de matemáticas en la primera parte del año. Su hijo/a ayudará a crear un borde con plantillas para el salón de clase y a planear una fiesta imaginaria para la clase. Su hijo/a utilizará muchos de los conceptos en los que hemos estado trabajando, como el método de laboratorio TIMS, el valor posicional, la suma, la resta, la multiplicación y la división. Se evaluará el trabajo para determinar la comprensión del contenido matemático, la resolución de problemas y la comunicación de soluciones.

Su hijo/a también tomará un examen de mitad de año para evaluar su conocimiento de los conceptos y las habilidades cubiertos en las primeras nueve unidades y otro examen para medir el progreso con las restas básicas. Finalmente, como parte de nuestro proceso de reflexión, su hijo/a dedicará un tiempo a revisar su portafolio de matemáticas. Hablaremos sobre el trabajo que su hijo/a ha hecho desde el comienzo del año.

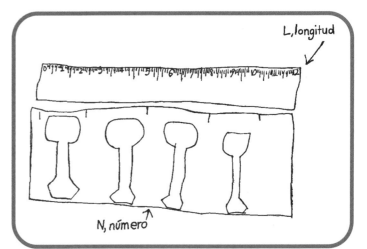

Dibujo de un niño para mostrar la longitud de un borde hecho con una plantilla

Mientras nosotros repasamos lo que su hijo/a ha aprendido en la clase de matemáticas, usted puede proporcionarle apoyo adicional haciendo actividades como las siguientes:

- Alentar a su hijo/a a llevar a casa cualquier juego de matemáticas que haya jugado. Cada juego es un método de repaso excelente.

- Pedirle a su hijo/a que lleve a casa su tabla de "Las tablas que conozco" sobre la resta. Ayudar a su hijo/a a repasar las restas básicas que le resulten difíciles. Animar a su hijo/a a hablar acerca de las distintas estrategias mentales que puede usar para acordarse de esas restas más fácilmente.

Gracias por su esfuerzo continuo para ayudar a su hijo/a con las ideas matemáticas a través de charlas y juegos.

Atentamente,

Table of Contents

Unit 10
Numbers and Patterns:
An Assessment Unit

Unit 10

Outline
Numbers and Patterns:
An Assessment Unit

Unit Summary

Estimated Class Sessions

6-8

The formal assessment activities in this unit, together with ongoing informal and formal assessment activities in the other units, help teachers monitor student progress. Paper-and-pencil problems and short tasks provide information about concepts and skills developed in Units 1–9. A review of student portfolios allows you to examine student progress since the beginning of the school year. Student work in designing and carrying out the lab, *Stencilrama,* enables you to assess many of the skills and concepts developed in preceding units. Students' abilities to communicate mathematical ideas are also assessed. The DPP for this unit first reviews and assesses the subtraction facts in Groups 7 and 8 and then assesses all the subtraction facts. DPP items also develop strategies for the last six multiplication facts (4×6, 4×7, 4×8, 6×7, 6×8, 7×8).

Major Concept Focus

- TIMS Laboratory Method
- measuring length in inches
- point graphs
- predicting
- checking predictions
- investigating patterns
- subtraction facts practice
- Game: subtraction facts
- money
- communicating problem-solving solutions
- assessing problem solving
- midyear test
- subtraction facts review and assessment for Groups 7 and 8
- assessment of all subtraction facts
- strategies for the last six multiplication facts

Pacing Suggestions

- Lessons in this unit provide review, application, and assessment of concepts and skills in Units 1–9. Students' abilities with these skills and concepts will determine how quickly they can move through the unit.
- Lesson 4 *Word Problems for Review* is an optional lesson. You can distribute the problems in that lesson for homework throughout the unit or students can work on them together in class.

Assessment Indicators

Use the following Assessment Indicators and the *Observational Assessment Record* that follows the Background section in this unit to assess students on key ideas.

A1. Can students measure length in inches?

A2. Can students identify and use variables?

A3. Can students collect, organize, graph, and analyze data?

A4. Can students use patterns in data tables and graphs to make predictions and solve problems?

A5. Can students solve open-response problems and communicate solution strategies?

A6. Do students demonstrate fluency with the subtraction facts in Groups 7 and 8?

A7. Do students demonstrate fluency with all the subtraction facts?

Unit Planner

KEY: SG = Student Guide, DAB = Discovery Assignment Book, AB = Adventure Book, URG = Unit Resource Guide, DPP = Daily Practice and Problems, HP = Home Practice (found in Discovery Assignment Book), and TIG = Teacher Implementation Guide.

	Lesson Information	Supplies	Copies/Transparencies

Lesson 1

Stencilrama

URG Pages 22–44
SG Pages 130–134
DAB Pages 147–150

DPP A–F
HP Parts 1–2

Estimated Class Sessions
3

Assessment Lab
Students make borders by using a stencil. They investigate the relationship between the number of stencils and the length of the border by collecting and graphing data. Then students use the data to make predictions and solve problems involving multiplication.

Math Facts
DPP Bits A and E provide practice with the subtraction facts in Groups 7 and 8. DPP Bit C encourages students to practice the subtraction facts in Group 7 using the *Subtraction Flash Cards*. Task F develops strategies for the multiplication facts.

Homework
1. Assign Home Practice Parts 1 and 2.
2. Assign the word problems in Lesson 4.
3. Students study the subtraction facts in Groups 7 and 8 at home using the flash cards.

Assessment
1. Use the *Observational Assessment Record* to document students' abilities to measure length in inches and to collect, organize, graph, and analyze data.
2. Add this lab to students' portfolios.
3. Score **Questions 5** and **6** using the *TIMS Multidimensional Rubric*.

Supplies:
- 1 3 × 5 inch index card per student group
- 1 pair of scissors per student group
- 1 ruler per student
- colored markers
- strips of paper approximately 36″ by 7″ or large paper grocery bags per student group
- 1 meterstick per student
- examples of designs from different cultures
- examples of stencils, optional

Copies/Transparencies:
- 1 copy of *Centimeter Graph Paper* URG Page 36 per student
- 1 copy of *Subtraction Flash Cards: Groups 7* and *8* URG Pages 37–40 per student, copied back-to-back, optional
- 1 copy of the *TIMS Multidimensional Rubric* TIG Assessment section
- 1 copy of the *Observational Assessment Record* URG Pages 9–10 to be used throughout this unit

Lesson 2

Problem Game

URG Pages 45–63
SG Page 135
DAB Pages 151–153

DPP G–H
HP Parts 3–4

Estimated Class Sessions
1

Game
Students review subtraction facts while playing a game.

Math Facts
DPP Bit G asks students to practice the subtraction facts in Group 8 using *Subtraction Flash Cards*.

Homework
1. Remind students to use their flash cards to study the subtraction facts.
2. Assign Home Practice Parts 3 and 4.

Supplies:
- 1 game token or centimeter connecting cube per student
- 1 clear plastic spinner or pencil with paper clip per student group

Copies/Transparencies:
- 1 copy of *Subtraction Flash Cards: Groups 1–8* URG Pages 37–40 and 51–62 per student, copied back-to-back

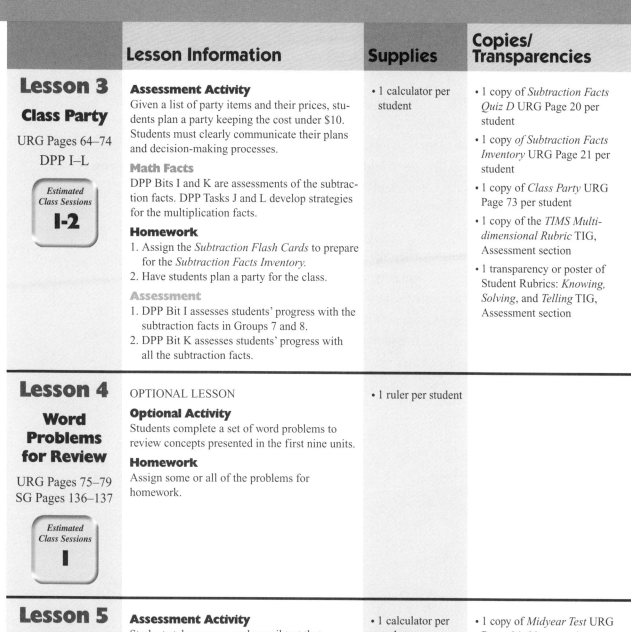

	Lesson Information	Supplies	Copies/Transparencies
Lesson 3 **Class Party** URG Pages 64–74 DPP I–L *Estimated Class Sessions* **1-2**	**Assessment Activity** Given a list of party items and their prices, students plan a party keeping the cost under $10. Students must clearly communicate their plans and decision-making processes. **Math Facts** DPP Bits I and K are assessments of the subtraction facts. DPP Tasks J and L develop strategies for the multiplication facts. **Homework** 1. Assign the *Subtraction Flash Cards* to prepare for the *Subtraction Facts Inventory.* 2. Have students plan a party for the class. **Assessment** 1. DPP Bit I assesses students' progress with the subtraction facts in Groups 7 and 8. 2. DPP Bit K assesses students' progress with all the subtraction facts.	• 1 calculator per student	• 1 copy of *Subtraction Facts Quiz D* URG Page 20 per student • 1 copy of *Subtraction Facts Inventory* URG Page 21 per student • 1 copy of *Class Party* URG Page 73 per student • 1 copy of the *TIMS Multidimensional Rubric* TIG, Assessment section • 1 transparency or poster of Student Rubrics: *Knowing, Solving,* and *Telling* TIG, Assessment section
Lesson 4 **Word Problems for Review** URG Pages 75–79 SG Pages 136–137 *Estimated Class Sessions* **1**	OPTIONAL LESSON **Optional Activity** Students complete a set of word problems to review concepts presented in the first nine units. **Homework** Assign some or all of the problems for homework.	• 1 ruler per student	
Lesson 5 **Midyear Test** URG Pages 80–93 DPP M–N *Estimated Class Sessions* **1**	**Assessment Activity** Students take a paper-and-pencil test that assesses concepts and skills studied in the first nine units. **Assessment** 1. Add students' tests to their portfolios. 2. Transfer documentation from the Unit 10 *Observational Assessment Record* to students' *Individual Assessment Record Sheets.*	• 1 calculator per student • 1 ruler per student	• 1 copy of *Midyear Test* URG Pages 84–90 per student • 1 copy of *Individual Assessment Record Sheet* TIG Assessment section per student, previously copied for use throughout the year

Connections

A current list of literature and software connections is available at *www.mathtrailblazers.com.* You can also find information on connections in the *Teacher Implementation Guide* Literature List and Software List sections.

Literature Connections
Suggested Titles
- Bartok, Mira. *West Africa: Nigeria.* Good Year Books, Parsipanny, NJ, 1994.
- Xiong, Blia. *Nine-in-One, Grr! Grr!* Children's Book Press, San Francisco, 1993. (Lesson 1)
- *West Africa: Ghana, Ancient Japan,* and *Ancient Mexico* from the Ancient and Living Cultures series. GoodYearBooks, Scott Foresman, Glenview, IL, 1993. (Lesson 1)

Software Connections
- *Graphers* is a data graphing tool appropriate for young students.
- *Ice Cream Truck* develops problem solving, money skills, and arithmetic operations.
- *Kid Pix* allows students to create their own illustrations.
- *Math Arena* is a collection of math activities that reinforces many math concepts.
- *Money Challenge* provides practice with money.
- *Number Facts Fire Zapper* provides practice with number facts in an arcade-like game.
- *Penny Pot* provides practice with counting coins.

Teaching All Math Trailblazers Students

Math Trailblazers® lessons are designed for students with a wide range of abilities. The lessons are flexible and do not require significant adaptation for diverse learning styles or academic levels. However, when needed, lessons can be tailored to allow students to engage their abilities to the greatest extent possible while building knowledge and skills.

To assist you in meeting the needs of all students in your classroom, this section contains information about some of the features in the curriculum that allow all students access to mathematics. For additional information, see the Teaching the *Math Trailblazers* Student: Meeting Individual Needs section in the *Teacher Implementation Guide.*

Differentiation Opportunities in this Unit

Games

Use games to promote or extend understanding of math concepts and to practice skills with children who need more practice.

- Lesson 2 *Problem Game*

Laboratory Experiments

Laboratory experiments enable students to solve problems using a variety of representations including pictures, tables, graphs, and symbols. Teachers can assign or adapt parts of the analysis according to the student's ability. The following lesson is a lab:

- Lesson 1 *Stencilrama*

Journal Prompts

Journal prompts provide opportunities for students to explain and reflect on mathematical problems. They can help both students who need practice explaining their ideas and students who benefit from answering higher order questions. Students with various learning styles can express themselves using pictures, words, and sentences. Teachers can alter journal prompts to suit students' ability levels. The following lessons contain a journal prompt:

- Lesson 1 *Stencilrama*
- Lesson 3 *Class Party*

DPP Challenges

DPP Challenges are items from the Daily Practice and Problems that usually take more than fifteen minutes to complete. These problems are more thought-provoking and can be used to stretch students' problem-solving skills. The following lessons have a DPP Challenge in them:

- DPP Challenge D from Lesson 1 *Stencilrama*
- DPP Challenge N from Lesson 5 *Midyear Test*

Extensions

Use extensions to enrich lessons. Many extensions provide opportunities to further involve or challenge students of all abilities. Take a moment to review the extensions prior to beginning this unit. Some extensions may require additional preparation and planning. The following lesson contains an extension:

- Lesson 4 *Word Problems for Review*

Unit 10

Background
Numbers and Patterns:
An Assessment Unit

This unit contains a variety of assessment items that can provide you with a range of information about students' mathematical knowledge. The activities and tests in this unit will give you a balanced picture of your students' progress since the beginning of the year. The results of these assessments will complement what you already know about students through daily observation of their abilities in the classroom.

Each activity in the unit will give you a different piece of information. As students work on the Stencilrama lab in Lesson 1, you can evaluate their abilities to complete a long task while working in a group. As students work together and you review their written responses, you can look for growth in their abilities to identify the variables in an investigation; to collect, organize, and graph data; and to use the data to make predictions and solve problems. Lesson 3 *Class Party* is a shorter task that will give you information on students' growth in solving problems and communicating mathematical ideas. These two activities are examples of assessments that should look and feel like instruction.

The two tests in this unit provide information on students' skills in addition, subtraction, measurement, and other concepts and procedures. Use Lesson 2 *Problem Game,* the *Subtraction Flash*

Cards, and Lesson 4 *Word Problems for Review* to help prepare your students for these tests. Students can study two groups of the *Subtraction Flash Cards* (Groups 1–8) every night for homework as review for the assessments. The end of this unit is an appropriate time to review students' portfolios, comparing work on activities in this unit to similar tasks from earlier units. See the TIMS Tutor: *Portfolios* in the *Teacher Implementation Guide* for information on how to organize and review the portfolios.

Besides the formal assessments included in this unit, you can use other features to determine students' progress. Use the *Observational Assessment Record* to keep track of progress, the Journal Prompts for a general review of their understanding and abilities to communicate mathematical ideas, and the three dimensions of the *TIMS Multidimensional Rubric* to score and evaluate students' work.

Resources

- National Council of Teachers of Mathematics. *Assessment Standards for School Mathematics.* Reston, VA, 1995.
- *Principles and Standards for School Mathematics.* National Council of Teachers of Mathematics, Reston, VA, 2000.

"To make effective decisions, teachers should look for convergence of evidence from different sources. Formal assessments provide only one viewpoint on what students can do in a very particular situation—often working individually on paper-and-pencil tasks, with limited time to complete the tasks. Overreliance on such assessments may give an incomplete and perhaps distorted picture of students' performance. Because different students show what they know and can do in different ways, assessments should allow for multiple approaches, thus giving a well-rounded picture and allowing each student to show his or her best strengths."

From the National Council of Teachers of Mathematics, *Principles and Standards for School Mathematics,* 2000, p. 23.

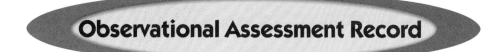

Observational Assessment Record

A1 Can students measure length in inches?

A2 Can students identify and use variables?

A3 Can students collect, organize, graph, and analyze data?

A4 Can students use patterns in data tables and graphs to make predictions and solve problems?

A5 Can students solve open-response problems and communicate solution strategies?

A6 Do students demonstrate fluency with the subtraction facts in Groups 7 and 8?

A7 Do students demonstrate fluency with all the subtraction facts?

A8 _____

Name	A1	A2	A3	A4	A5	A6	A7	A8	Comments
1.									
2.									
3.									
4.									
5.									
6.									
7.									
8.									
9.									
10.									
11.									
12.									
13.									

Name	A1	A2	A3	A4	A5	A6	A7	A8	Comments
14.									
15.									
16.									
17.									
18.									
19.									
20.									
21.									
22.									
23.									
24.									
25.									
26.									
27.									
28.									
29.									
30.									
31.									
32.									

Unit 10

Daily Practice and Problems
Numbers and Patterns:
An Assessment Unit

A DPP Menu for Unit 10

Two Daily Practice and Problems (DPP) items are included for each class session listed in the Unit Outline. A scope and sequence chart for the DPP is in the *Teacher Implementation Guide*.

Icons in the Teacher Notes column designate the subject matter of each DPP item. The first item in each class session is always a Bit and the second is either a Task or Challenge. Each item falls into one or more of the categories listed below. A menu of the DPP items for Unit 10 follows.

N Number Sense	Computation	Time	Geometry
D	B, D, F, N	M	H

$\frac{5}{\times 7}$ Math Facts	$ Money	Measurement	Data
A, C, E–G, I–L		H	

Practicing and Assessing the Subtraction Facts

In this unit students review and are assessed on the subtraction facts in Groups 7 and 8 and then assessed on all 72 subtraction facts in Groups 1–8.

DPP Bits C and G remind students to use their *Subtraction Flash Cards: Groups 7 and 8.* DPP Bits A and E provide practice with the facts in these groups. *Subtraction Facts Quiz D* is in DPP Bit I. Students should update their *Subtraction Facts I Know* charts after taking the quiz. Students will continue to practice the subtraction facts daily as they solve problems in activities, investigations, and labs.

To prepare for the *Subtraction Facts Inventory,* in DPP Bit K, students should study their flash cards. You can make extra copies of the flash cards using the masters found in Lesson 1. Tell students when the test will be given and encourage them to study the facts at home. They can also study by playing

games that review the subtraction facts. (See Lesson Guide 2 for a list of the games.)

Developing Strategies for the Multiplication Facts

DPP items in this unit continue to develop strategies for the multiplication facts. The last six facts are targeted in this unit: $4 \times 6, 4 \times 7, 4 \times 8, 6 \times 7, 6 \times 8, 7 \times 8$. See DPP items F, J, and L for work with these facts.

For information on the practice and assessment of subtraction facts in Grade 3, see the Lesson Guide for Unit 2 Lesson 7 *Assessing the Subtraction Facts.* For information on the study of the multiplication facts in Grade 3, see the DPP Guides for Units 3 and 11. For a detailed explanation of our approach to learning and assessing the math facts in Grade 3, see the *Grade 3 Facts Resource Guide,* and for information for Grades K–5, see the TIMS Tutor: *Math Facts* in the *Teacher Implementation Guide.*

 **Daily Practice and Problems**

Students may solve the items individually, in groups, or as a class. The items may also be assigned for homework. The DPPs are also available on the Teacher Resource CD.

Student Questions	Teacher Notes

 Subtraction Facts: Group 7

Do these problems in your head. Write only the answers.

1. $14 - 7 =$

2. $14 - 8 =$

3. $14 - 6 =$

4. $12 - 6 =$

5. $12 - 7 =$

6. $12 - 5 =$

7. $13 - 6 =$

8. $13 - 7 =$

9. $10 - 5 =$

TIMS Bit

To focus practice on these facts, students can work with *Subtraction Flash Cards: Group 7*. Students can use the flash cards to study for *Subtraction Facts Quiz D* in Bit I, which has facts from Groups 7 and 8. Ask students to describe strategies they use. They can use doubles and reason from known facts (doubles) to solve these facts. TIMS Bits E and G review Group 8. Students will take an inventory test on Groups 1–8 in Bit K.

1. 7   2. 6   3. 8
4. 6   5. 5   6. 7
7. 7   8. 6   9. 5

B **Subtraction with Zeros**

Complete the following problems. Use pencil and paper or mental math to find the answers.

1. 6000
    − 350

2. 7005
    −2333

3. 900
    − 567

4. 8000
    − 199

5. 301
    − 87

6. 5000
    − 3999

7. Explain a way to do Question 6 in your head.

TIMS Task

1. 5650

2. 4672

3. 333

4. 7801

5. 214

6. 1001

7. Possible strategy: Students can count up one from 3999 to 4000 and then to 5000 by 1000.

C **Subtraction Flash Cards: Group 7**

1. With a partner, sort the Flash Cards for Group 7 into three stacks: Facts I Know Quickly, Facts I Know Using a Strategy, and Facts I Need to Learn.

2. Update your *Subtraction Facts I Know* chart. Circle the facts you answered quickly. Underline those you know by using a strategy. Do nothing to those you still need to learn.

TIMS Bit

Have students sort *Subtraction Flash Cards* for *Group 7*. After students sort, they should update the *Subtraction Facts I Know* charts. Students can take the cards for Group 7 home to practice with their families. The flash cards for Group 7 were distributed in the *Discovery Assignment Book* in Unit 5. They are also available in Lesson 1 and in the *Grade 3 Facts Resource Guide*.

Tell students when you will give *Subtraction Facts Quiz D*, which is made up of facts from Groups 7 and 8. Quiz D is at the end of this set of DPP items, following Item N. The quiz is assigned in Bit I.

D **Biggest and Smallest Sums**

Put a digit (1, 2, 3, 4, 5, 6, 7, 8, 9, or 0) in each box. Use each digit once or not at all.

What is the biggest sum you can get?

What is the smallest sum you can get?

What if a digit can be used more than once?

TIMS Challenge

The largest sum is
$9753 + 8642 = 18,395$.
The smallest sum is
$1046 + 2357 = 3403$
(or $1357 + 0246 = 1603$ if leading zeros are allowed). Other addends may give the same sums and are also correct.

If repeated digits are allowed, the largest sum is
$9999 + 9999 = 19,998$.
The smallest sum is
$1000 + 1000 = 2000$.

If leading zeros are allowed, the smallest sum is
$0000 + 0000 = 0$.

Student Questions	Teacher Notes

E Subtraction Facts: Group 8

Do these problems in your head. Write only the answers.

1. $16 - 8 =$ 2. $17 - 8 =$

3. $15 - 8 =$ 4. $18 - 9 =$

5. $18 - 10 =$ 6. $15 - 7 =$

7. $8 - 4 =$ 8. $7 - 4 =$

9. $6 - 3 =$

TIMS Bit

Students can study this group of facts with the flash cards for Group 8, discussing the strategies they use to remember them. Tell students when you will give *Subtraction Facts Quiz D*, which is made up of facts from Groups 7 and 8. Quiz D is at the end of this set of DPP items, following item N. The quiz is assigned in Bit I.

1. 8   2. 9

3. 7   4. 9

5. 8   6. 8

7. 4   8. 3

9. 3

F Masses

Suppose we use these standard masses to measure mass using a two-pan balance: 8-gram masses, 4-gram masses, and 1-gram masses. How many of each would you need to use to balance an apple with a mass of 62 grams? Find as many solutions as you can.

TIMS Task

There are many solutions to the problem and many ways to find and express answers. Here are two possibilities:

$7 \times 8\,g + 6 \times 1\,g = 62\,g$

$5 \times 8\,g + 5 \times 4\,g + 2 \times 1\,g = 62\,g$

G Subtraction Flash Cards: Group 8

1. With a partner, sort the Flash Cards for Group 8 into three stacks: Facts I Know Quickly, Facts I Know Using a Strategy, and Facts I Need to Learn.

2. Update your *Subtraction Facts I Know* chart. Circle the facts you answered quickly. Underline those you know by using a strategy. Do nothing to those you still need to learn.

TIMS Bit

Have students sort *Subtraction Flash Cards: Group 8*. After students sort, they should update the *Subtraction Facts I Know* charts. Students can take the cards for Group 8 home to practice with their families. The flash cards for Group 8 were distributed in the *Discovery Assignment Book* in Unit 5. They are also available in Lesson 1 and in the *Grade 3 Facts Resource Guide*.

Students can study this group of facts with the flash cards for Group 7, discussing the strategies they use to remember them. Tell students when you will give *Subtraction Facts Quiz D*, which is made up of facts from Groups 7 and 8. Quiz D is at the end of this set of DPP items, following Item N. The quiz is assigned in Bit I.

H Spot

Boo the Blob has a dog named Spot. Find Spot's area.

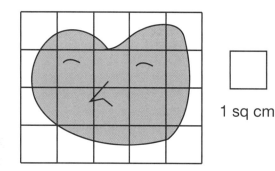

1 sq cm

TIMS Task

Approximately 11 sq cm

Student Questions	Teacher Notes

I **Subtraction Facts Quiz D**

Students take *Subtraction Facts Quiz D,* which corresponds to *Subtraction Flash Cards: Groups 7* and *8.*

TIMS Bit

Quiz D is at the end of this set of DPP items. Ask students to have two pens or pencils of different colors ready. During the first minute of the quiz, they should write their answers using one color pen or pencil. After you tell students that a minute has passed, they should begin writing their answers with the other color pen or pencil. After students have been given a reasonable amount of time to complete the rest of the problems, they should check their work. Students should update their *Subtraction Facts I Know* charts using the results of the quiz.

DPP Bit K is an inventory test on all the subtraction facts. Encourage students to study for the test using their flash cards. Students should concentrate on those facts that are not yet marked on their *Subtraction Facts I Know* charts.

J **Moe and Joe Smart**

1. Moe Smart is helping his brother Joe with his homework. Joe says, "Seven times eight is 54." How can Moe show Joe he is wrong?

2. Joe Smart says, "Six times eight is 46." How can Moe show Joe he is wrong?

TIMS Task

Students can use manipulatives or drawings to show that $8 \times 7 = 56$ and $6 \times 8 = 48$.

K Subtraction Facts Inventory

Students take an inventory test of the 72 subtraction facts that were studied in Groups 1–8 throughout Units 2–10.

TIMS Bit

The *Subtraction Facts Inventory* is at the end of this set of DPP items. Ask students to have two pens or pencils of different colors ready. During the first four minutes of the test, students should write their answers using one color pen or pencil. After four minutes, students should begin writing their answers with the other color pen or pencil. Give students a reasonable amount of time to finish the test.

L Double Doubles

1. $2 \times 6 =$

2. $2 \times 2 \times 6 =$

3. $4 \times 6 =$

4. $2 \times 7 =$

5. $2 \times 2 \times 7 =$

6. $4 \times 7 =$

7. $2 \times 8 =$

8. $2 \times 2 \times 8 =$

9. $4 \times 8 =$

10. $3 \times 7 =$

11. $2 \times 3 \times 7 =$

12. $6 \times 7 =$

13. $3 \times 8 =$

14. $2 \times 3 \times 8 =$

15. $6 \times 8 =$

TIMS Task

Ask students to describe patterns that will help them learn these facts.

1. 12	2. 24
3. 24	4. 14
5. 28	6. 28
7. 16	8. 32
9. 32	10. 21
11. 42	12. 42
13. 24	14. 48
15. 48	

Student Questions	Teacher Notes

(M) Time

What time is it now?

What time was it a half hour ago?

What time will it be in a half hour?

How long will it be until school is out?

TIMS Bit 🕐

Answers will vary.

(N) Wheels, Wheels, Wheels

In Felicia's garage, there are lots of things with wheels. One day she counted all the wheels: There were 24. Felicia made up a puzzle for her friend Alex. She said, "Alex, there are 24 wheels in my garage. There might be tricycles, bicycles, or wagons. What do you think I have in my garage?"

1. Guess what Felicia has in her garage.

2. Can you know for sure? Explain your answer.

TIMS Challenge ▨

Possible solutions: 6 wagons, 8 tricycles, 12 bikes, 3 wagons and 4 tricycles, 2 wagons and 2 tricycles and 5 bikes, etc.

This problem has many correct answers. The abundance of possibilities suggests that Felicia should give Alex more hints. Ask students to think of more hints to give Alex.

Name _____   Date _____

Subtraction Facts Quiz D

You will need two pens or pencils of different colors. Use the first color when you begin the test. When your teacher tells you to switch pens or pencils, finish the test using the second color.

14	16	12	6	14	13
− 7	− 8	− 7	− 3	− 8	− 6

12	14	13	10	18	7
− 6	− 6	− 7	− 5	− 10	− 4

8	12	15	17	15	18
− 4	− 5	− 7	− 8	− 8	− 9

Teacher: These facts correspond with *Subtraction Flash Cards*: *Groups 7* and *8.*

Assessment Blackline Master

Subtraction Facts Inventory

You will need two pens or pencils of different colors. Use the first color when you begin the test. When your teacher tells you to switch pens or pencils, finish the test using the second color.

9 − 2	11 − 9	7 − 3	16 − 7	11 − 4	11 − 2	7 − 4	14 − 10
10 − 2	14 − 7	16 − 9	12 − 4	13 − 7	11 − 5	8 − 2	4 − 2
10 − 8	11 − 7	13 − 10	8 − 6	5 − 3	13 − 8	12 − 10	16 − 8
9 − 3	7 − 5	6 − 2	11 − 6	17 − 9	10 − 3	13 − 5	16 − 10
14 − 5	15 − 7	10 − 6	9 − 5	11 − 3	13 − 6	8 − 5	12 − 7
5 − 2	12 − 8	9 − 4	12 − 9	10 − 7	12 − 3	9 − 6	10 − 5
13 − 4	8 − 3	15 − 6	17 − 10	18 − 9	14 − 9	17 − 8	6 − 3
19 − 10	15 − 8	15 − 10	6 − 4	11 − 8	13 − 9	9 − 7	15 − 9
14 − 6	12 − 6	14 − 8	18 − 10	10 − 4	8 − 4	12 − 5	7 − 2

Lesson 1

Stencilrama

Lesson Overview

Estimated Class Sessions

3

Students cut a stencil into an index card and make a pattern by repeatedly using the stencil on a long piece of paper to create a border, such as the one shown in Figure 1. The borders can be used to decorate a room. Following the TIMS Laboratory Method, students investigate the relationship between the number of times they use the stencil and the length of the resulting border. They collect, organize, and graph data about the length of borders using the stencil a small number of times. Then students look for patterns in the data to help them make predictions and solve problems about longer borders that require multiplication.

Figure 1: *A border made using a stencil*

Key Content

- Measuring length in inches.
- Collecting, organizing, graphing, and analyzing data.
- Using patterns in tables and graphs to make predictions and solve problems.
- Using data to solve problems involving multiplication.
- Developing multiplication facts strategies.
- Solving open-response problems and communicating solution strategies.

Key Vocabulary

- stencil

Math Facts

DPP Bits A and E provide practice with the subtraction facts in Groups 7 and 8. DPP Bit C encourages students to practice the subtraction facts in Group 7 using the *Subtraction Flash Cards*. Task F develops strategies for the multiplication facts.

Homework

1. Assign Home Practice Parts 1 and 2.
2. Assign the word problems in Lesson 4.
3. Students study the subtraction facts in Groups 7 and 8 at home using the flash cards.

Assessment

1. Use the *Observational Assessment Record* to document students' abilities to measure length in inches and to collect, organize, graph, and analyze data.
2. Add this lab to students' portfolios.
3. Score **Questions 5** and **6** using the *TIMS Multidimensional Rubric*.

Curriculum Sequence

Before This Unit

Assessment Lab

This lab assesses whether students can identify variables in an experiment, measure length, and collect and organize data. Students also use a graph to make predictions and solve problems involving multiplication. To complete this assessment lab, students will need to use many of the skills and concepts they have studied since the beginning of the school year.

It assesses these concepts and skills in the context of an investigation students work on for several days. The following labs or activities have prepared students for the work in this unit: *Kind of Bean* (Unit 1), *Spinning Differences* (Unit 2), *The Better "Picker Upper"* (Unit 5), *Lemonade Stand* (Unit 7), *Walking around Shapes* (Unit 7), and *Mass vs. Number* (Unit 9).

After This Unit

Assessment Lab

Students will continue to use the TIMS Laboratory Method as a tool for developing concepts and skills. Students will measure volume and apply multiplication and division in Unit 16 Lesson 2 *Fill 'er Up.*

They will develop decimal concepts in Unit 15 Lesson 4 *Length vs. Number.* Lesson 2 Tower Power in Unit 20 is a final assessment lab that will provide an opportunity to document students' growth in third grade.

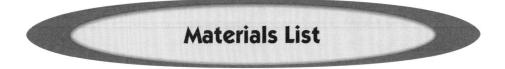

Materials List

Supplies and Copies

Student	Teacher
Supplies for Each Student • ruler • colored markers • meterstick **Supplies for Each Student Group** • 1 3 × 5 inch index card • scissors • strips of paper approximately 36″ by 7″ or large paper grocery bags	**Supplies** • examples of designs from different cultures • examples of stencils, optional
Copies • 1 copy of *Centimeter Graph Paper* per student (*Unit Resource Guide* Page 36) • 1 copy of *Subtraction Flash Cards: Groups 7 and 8* per student copied back-to-back, optional (*Unit Resource Guide* Pages 37–40)	**Copies/Transparencies** • 1 copy of *Observational Assessment Record* to be used throughout this unit (*Unit Resource Guide* Pages 9–10)

All blackline masters including assessment, transparency, and DPP masters are also on the Teacher Resource CD.

Student Books

Stencilrama (*Student Guide* Pages 130–134)
Stencilrama (*Discovery Assignment Book* Pages 147–150)
Student Rubrics: *Knowing, Solving,* and *Telling* (*Student Guide* Appendices A, B, and C and Inside Back Cover)

Daily Practice and Problems and Home Practice

DPP items A–F (*Unit Resource Guide* Pages 12–15)
Home Practice Parts 1–2 (*Discovery Assignment Book* Page 144)

Note: Classrooms whose pacing differs significantly from the suggested pacing of the units should use the Math Facts Calendar in Section 4 of the *Facts Resource Guide* to ensure students receive the complete math facts program.

Assessment Tools

Observational Assessment Record (*Unit Resource Guide* Pages 9–10)
TIMS Multidimensional Rubric (*Teacher Implementation Guide,* Assessment section)

Daily Practice and Problems

Suggestions for using the DPPs are on page 32.

A. Bit: Subtraction Facts: Group 7

(URG p. 12)

Do these problems in your head. Write only the answers.

1. $14 - 7 =$
2. $14 - 8 =$
3. $14 - 6 =$
4. $12 - 6 =$
5. $12 - 7 =$
6. $12 - 5 =$
7. $13 - 6 =$
8. $13 - 7 =$
9. $10 - 5 =$

B. Task: Subtraction with Zeros

(URG p. 13)

Complete the following problems. Use pencil and paper or mental math to find the answers.

1. $\begin{array}{r} 6000 \\ -\ 350 \end{array}$
2. $\begin{array}{r} 7005 \\ -\ 2333 \end{array}$
3. $\begin{array}{r} 900 \\ -\ 567 \end{array}$
4. $\begin{array}{r} 8000 \\ -\ 199 \end{array}$
5. $\begin{array}{r} 301 \\ -\ 87 \end{array}$
6. $\begin{array}{r} 5000 \\ -\ 3999 \end{array}$

7. Explain a way to do Question 6 in your head.

C. Bit: Subtraction Flash Cards: Group 7 (URG p. 14)

1. With a partner, sort the Flash Cards for Group 7 into three stacks: Facts I Know Quickly, Facts I Know Using a Strategy, and Facts I Need to Learn.
2. Update your *Subtraction Facts I Know* chart. Circle the facts you answered quickly. Underline those you know by using a strategy. Do nothing to those you still need to learn.

D. Challenge: Biggest and Smallest Sums (URG p. 14)

Put a digit (1, 2, 3, 4, 5, 6, 7, 8, 9, or 0) in each box. Use each digit once or not at all.

$$\square\square\square\square + \square\square\square\square =$$

What is the biggest sum you can get?

What is the smallest sum you can get?

What if a digit can be used more than once?

E. Bit: Subtraction Facts: Group 8

(URG p. 15)

Do these problems in your head. Write only the answers.

1. $16 - 8 =$
2. $17 - 8 =$
3. $15 - 8 =$
4. $18 - 9 =$
5. $18 - 10 =$
6. $15 - 7 =$
7. $8 - 4 =$
8. $7 - 4 =$
9. $6 - 3 =$

F. Task: Masses (URG p. 15)

Suppose we use these standard masses to measure mass using a two-pan balance: 8-gram masses, 4-gram masses, and 1-gram masses. How many of each would you need to use to balance an apple with a mass of 62 grams? Find as many solutions as you can.

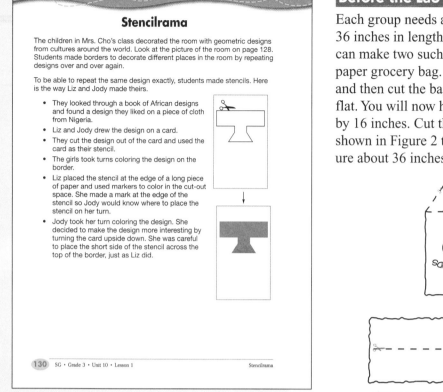

Stencilrama

The children in Mrs. Cho's class decorated the room with geometric designs from cultures around the world. Look at the picture of the room on page 128. Students made borders to decorate different places in the room by repeating designs over and over again.

To be able to repeat the same design exactly, students made stencils. Here is the way Liz and Jody made theirs.

- They looked through a book of African designs and found a design they liked on a piece of cloth from Nigeria.
- Liz and Jody drew the design on a card.
- They cut the design out of the card and used the card as their stencil.
- The girls took turns coloring the design on the border.
- Liz placed the stencil at the edge of a long piece of paper and used markers to color in the cut-out space. She made a mark at the edge of the stencil so Jody would know where to place the stencil on her turn.
- Jody took her turn coloring the design. She decided to make the design more interesting by turning the card upside down. She was careful to place the short side of the stencil across the top of the border, just as Liz did.

Student Guide - page 130

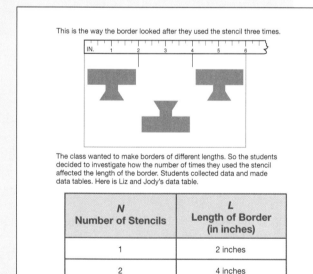

This is the way the border looked after they used the stencil three times.

The class wanted to make borders of different lengths. So the students decided to investigate how the number of times they used the stencil affected the length of the border. Students collected data and made data tables. Here is Liz and Jody's data table.

N Number of Stencils	L Length of Border (in inches)
1	2 inches
2	4 inches
4	8 inches

This data table reminded students of the data table they made for *Lemonade Stand*. They remembered how they used a graph of that data to make predictions about the number of lemons in a pitcher of lemonade.

Student Guide - page 131

Each group needs a piece of paper approximately 36 inches in length to make a border design. You can make two such strips of paper from one large paper grocery bag. Cut the bottom out of the bag and then cut the bag so the paper will open and lie flat. You will now have a rectangle about 36 inches by 16 inches. Cut the rectangle down the middle as shown in Figure 2 to create two rectangles that measure about 36 inches by 8 inches.

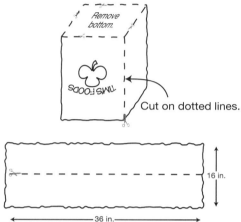

Figure 2: *Cutting a paper bag to make two long pieces of paper*

Gather examples of multicultural patterned designs to help inspire students in Part 2 of the lab. The local library or museum may help you gather artifacts that display repeated pattern designs. See the Resources section of this Lesson Guide for a list of books.

Teaching the Lab

Part 1 Launching the Investigation

Read and discuss the *Stencilrama* Lab Pages in the *Student Guide*. These pages begin by describing the process of making a border using stencils. Two girls in a classroom choose a design for a stencil, cut the stencil, and take turns using the stencil to start their border. The class wants to make borders of different lengths, so they decide to investigate how the number of times they use a stencil affects the length of the border. They collect data, record it in a data table, and make a graph.

Discuss the variables in the investigation using *Questions 1–4* in the *Student Guide*. *Question 1* asks what variables the two girls compared in their data table. These are the two main variables in the investigation: the Number of Stencils (N) and the Length

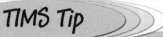
of the Border (*L*). ***Question 2*** asks what stayed the same as they made the border. This question is asking for the fixed variables. In order to look for the relationship between the number of times a stencil is used and the length of the border, the size and shape of the stencil must stay the same, there must not be any space between the stencils, and the orientation of the cards (either vertical or horizontal) must be the same each time. See Figure 3.

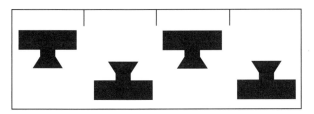

Figure 3: *Each time students used the stencil, they placed the index card vertically and marked the paper at the edge of the stencil.*

Question 3 asks what the two girls did to collect the data. They used the stencil four times, then measuring the distance between their marks, found the length of one, two, and four stencils. ***Question 4*** asks students what they need to know to find the number of times they would use the stencil to make a border across the top of the board. Since they predict the number of stencils, they need to measure the length of the board.

Part 2 Making a Stencil and Drawing the Picture

At this point, make a stencil from an index card as a sample. Model the procedure of making a border across a long piece of paper by using a stencil four times, marking the paper at the edge of the stencil. Point out those variables that need to be kept fixed. Tell students they will compare the number of stencils and the length of the border by measuring the length in inches of one, two, and four stencils just as the girls did in the vignette on the *Stencilrama* Lab Pages in the *Student Guide.*

So, the girls decided to make a graph of their stencil data. They used the graph to predict the number of stencils they needed for a border the length of Mrs. Cho's desk.

Let's say that your class decided to decorate your classroom using borders made with stencils. You will need to solve some problems. Here are some questions to discuss about Liz and Jody's data.

1. What variables did Liz and Jody compare in their data table?
2. What stayed the same as they made their borders?
3. What did Liz and Jody do to collect the data they wrote in their data table?
4. Suppose Liz and Jody wanted to make a border across the top of the blackboard. What would they need to know to find the number of times they will use the stencil?

Some Designs from Cultures of the World

Below are designs found on objects from different cultures. Also included is one type of stencil you might make from the design.

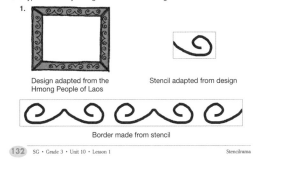

1.

Design adapted from the Hmong People of Laos

Stencil adapted from design

Border made from stencil

Student Guide - page 132 *(Answers on p. 41)*

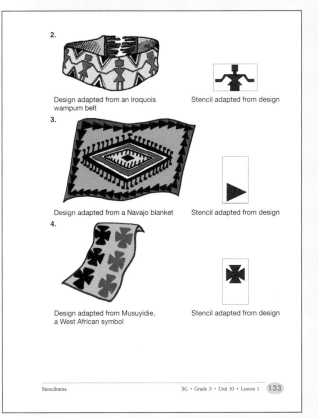

2.

Design adapted from an Iroquois wampum belt

Stencil adapted from design

3.

Design adapted from a Navajo blanket

Stencil adapted from design

4.

Design adapted from Musuyidie, a West African symbol

Stencil adapted from design

Student Guide - page 133

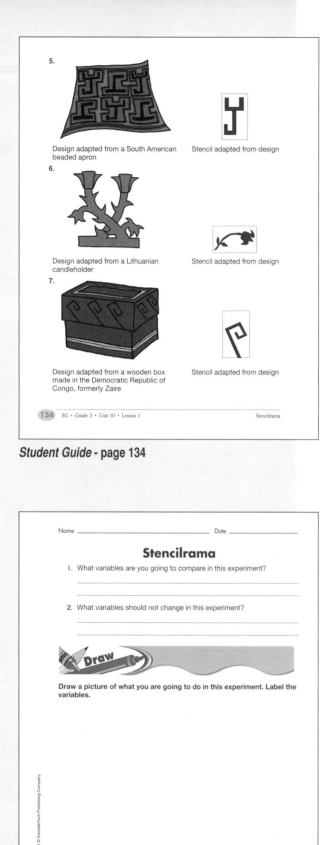

Student Guide - page 134

Discovery Assignment Book - page 147 *(Answers on p. 42)*

Each group should then choose a design and cut out a stencil. Groups can get ideas for their stencils from the examples shown in the section entitled Some Designs from Cultures of the World in the *Student Guide* or from books or objects in the classroom.

After each group cuts out a stencil, remind them that they are going to solve problems involving the number of stencils and their length. Have students draw a picture of the lab on the *Stencilrama* Lab Pages from the *Discovery Assignment Book*. Students should label the variables and show the procedure for making and measuring the border. Two student pictures are shown in Figure 4. In both pictures, students clearly labeled the variables of length and number. Students also indicated they will make small marks after they use the stencil each time so they will not leave any gaps between stencils. Nick's picture shows he will hold his index card vertically each time he uses the stencil. Sevara's picture shows she will always hold hers horizontally.

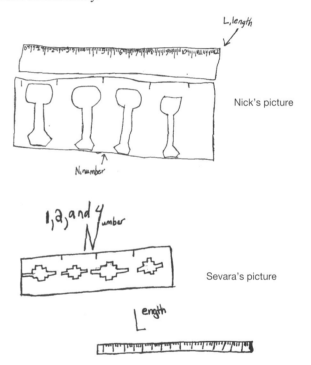

Figure 4: *Nick's and Sevara's pictures*

As you assess each drawing, check to see that students:

*   label the variables;
*   show the procedure for making and measuring the border; and
*   indicate that the unit of measure is inches.

Part 3 Collecting and Recording the Data

Students are now ready to measure the lengths of one, two, and four stencils and record the data on the *Stencilrama* Lab Pages in the *Discovery Assignment Book*. A sample data table is shown in Figure 5.

N Number of Stencils	L Length of Border (in inches)
1	3
2	6
4	12

Figure 5: *A sample data table for* Stencilrama

Students can fill in the last row with another number of stencils if they wish. Note that the data recorded here is correct if students placed the stencil on the paper vertically each time. The data will not always be this exact. There may be measurement error or students may have left some space between the stencils. A small amount of error is acceptable.

Encourage students to look for patterns in the data table. Many students see that as the number of stencils doubles, the length doubles as well. They also notice that the lengths are multiples of three, expressing it as "going by threes." (If the stencil is placed horizontally, the length should be multiples of five.)

Part 4 Graphing the Data

At this point, students should begin to make decisions within their groups (with only a little advice from you), so you can assess their abilities to make a graph and use it to solve problems. Students should decide how to label and scale the graph. The lab's directions tell students to make a point graph of their data, but let them decide if they should draw a line through the points. Each child should produce his or her own graph. A sample student graph is shown in Figure 6.

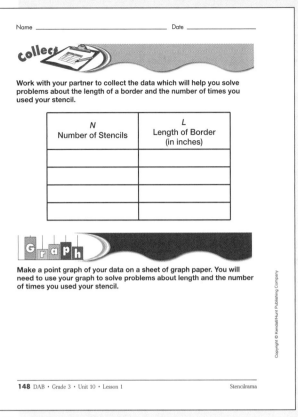

148 DAB • Grade 3 • Unit 10 • Lesson 1   Stencilrama

Discovery Assignment Book - page 148 *(Answers on p. 43)*

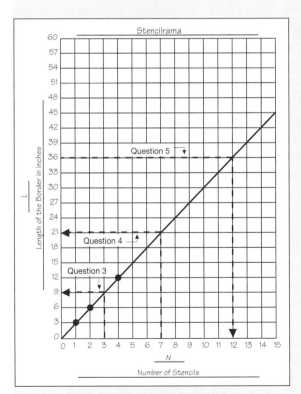

Figure 6: *Sample student graph*

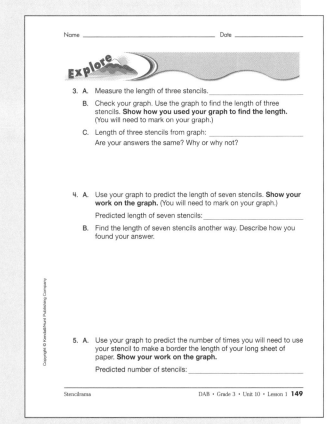

Name _____ Date _____

Explore

3. A. Measure the length of three stencils. _____

   B. Check your graph. Use the graph to find the length of three stencils. **Show how you used your graph to find the length.** (You will need to mark on your graph.)

   C. Length of three stencils from graph: _____
      Are your answers the same? Why or why not?

4. A. Use your graph to predict the length of seven stencils. **Show your work on the graph.** (You will need to mark on your graph.)

      Predicted length of seven stencils: _____

   B. Find the length of seven stencils another way. Describe how you found your answer.

5. A. Use your graph to predict the number of times you will need to use your stencil to make a border the length of your long sheet of paper. **Show your work on the graph.**

      Predicted number of stencils: _____

Stencilrama   DAB • Grade 3 • Unit 10 • Lesson 1 **149**

Discovery Assignment Book - page 149 *(Answers on p. 43)*

As you assess each graph, check to see that:

- the graph has a title;
- the axes are scaled and labeled appropriately;
- the points are plotted correctly; and
- the line is drawn accurately.

Also, be sure students have indicated on the graph how they used the line to make predictions for *Questions 3–5.*

Part 5 Solving the Problems

Students use the data table and graph to answer *Questions 3–5* on the *Stencilrama* Lab Pages in the *Discovery Assignment Book.* Remind students to use the three student rubrics to guide their work. Be sure students show how they found their answers on the graph so you can assess their abilities to use the graph to make predictions. See Figure 6.

Question 3 asks students to measure the length of three stencils and to find the length of three stencils using the graph. Both answers should be the same. If not, there is probably a mistake in the graph. Students should recognize any such problems at this time and decide to correct their graphs or make new ones.

Question 4 asks students to predict the length of seven stencils using the graph. After students use the graph to solve the problem, they are asked to solve the problem a different way. At this point, you can assess their abilities to solve a problem and communicate the solution. The following questions may guide you in assessing their written work.

- Did students use number sentences to represent the problem?
- Did students clearly show their problem-solving strategies?
- Did they connect the problem with multiplication?

Question 5 is more challenging. To use the graph to predict the number of stencils needed to make a border the length of the paper, students will need to measure the exact length of their papers (about 36 inches long). To check their predictions, some students might use their index cards to count the number of stencils it would take, while others might write number sentences using multiplication or division.

Question 6 may be the most interesting. The problem asks them to find the number of stencils it will take to make a border the length of some object in the room or the length of the room itself. Note that there is a blank at the end of the problem. You and your students can choose something in the room to decorate with a border and fill in the blank (e.g., the top of the door, the length of the board, the perimeter of the bulletin board).

The following samples of student work show they can solve the problem in many ways with varying levels of sophistication in problem-solving strategies and computational accuracy.

Liz's solution:

We took our stencil and went across the board with the stencil and we came up with $47\frac{1}{2}$.

Armando's solution:

$3\frac{1}{2}$ of my pieces of paper go on the board. 12 on each piece. $3 \times 12 = 36 + \frac{1}{2}$ (of 12) = 42 I took the bag and put it on the board and moved it across and the answer is 42.

Sevara's solution:

We measured the board with yardsticks [metersticks]. We figured out that $3 \times 39 + 25 = 142$ and then we figured out $142 \div 5 = 28$ R2. (Note: Sevara's stencil measured 5 inches and she used a meterstick, which is 39 inches long.)

Nick's solution:

First, I measured one side vertically, which is $73\frac{1}{4}$ inches. Then, I multiplied it by 2, which is $146\frac{1}{2}$ inches. Next, I measured another side horizontally, which was $99\frac{1}{2}$ inches. I multiplied it by 2, which was $208\frac{1}{2}$ inches. I added $208\frac{1}{2}$ inches and $146\frac{1}{2}$ inches and got 355 inches. Lastly, I divided 355 inches by 3 inches, and got 115 stencils. I used my calculator.

Questions 5 and *6* provide you with opportunities to assess students' work using all three dimensions of the *TIMS Multidimensional Rubric:* Knowing, Solving, and Telling. Use the following questions

Name _____ Date _____

B. Solve the problem another way to check. Tell how you solved the problem.

6. A. Find the number of times you will need to use your stencil to make a border across the _____. (Write the name of something you could decorate with a border in the blank. Your teacher will help you choose.)

B. Describe how you solved the problem.

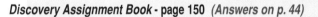

150 DAB • Grade 3 • Unit 10 • Lesson 1   Stencilrama

Discovery Assignment Book - **page 150** (Answers on p. 44)

Discovery Assignment Book - page 144 *(Answers on p. 42)*

along with the *TIMS Multidimensional Rubric* to assess students' work.

- Can students use the graph as a tool for solving problems?
- Did students measure to find the length of the object?
- Did students use drawings and number sentences to represent the problem?
- Did students clearly describe effective problem-solving strategies?
- Did students compute accurately?

Math Facts

- DPP Bits A and E provide practice with the subtraction facts in Groups 7 and 8. Bit C asks students to practice the subtraction facts in Group 7 using the *Subtraction Flash Cards.* For DPP Task F students can use multiplication facts (the last six facts) to solve a word problem.
- Home Practice Part 1 provides practice with the subtraction facts in Groups 7 and 8.

Homework and Practice

- For DPP Task B, students practice subtracting multidigit numbers involving zeros. DPP Challenge D provides practice with addition and builds number sense.
- Assign *Word Problems for Review* (Lesson 4) for homework.
- Ask students to use their *Subtraction Flash Cards: Groups 7* and *8* to practice at home with their families.
- For Home Practice Part 2, students subtract multidigit numbers.

Answers for Parts 1 and 2 of the Home Practice are in the Answer Key at the end of this lesson and at the end of this unit.

Assessment

- Use the *Observational Assessment Record* to document students' abilities to collect, organize, graph, and analyze data and measure length in inches.
- Use **Questions 5** and **6** to assess students' abilities to solve problems and communicate solution strategies using the *TIMS Multidimensional Rubric.*
- Add this lab to students' portfolios so you can compare students' performance on this lab to their performance on *Spinning Differences* in Unit 2 and future labs.

Literature Connections

- Xiong, Blia. *Nine-in-One, Grr! Grr!* Children's Book Press, San Francisco, 1993.

This book is a retelling of a folktale of the Hmong people of Laos. Each page is illustrated with a drawing adapted from Hmong needlework. The drawings are surrounded by borders that students can use as examples for their borders.

The book tells the story of a tiger who is promised nine cubs every year by the great god Shao. The other animals are worried that there will be too many tigers on Earth, so they change the promise to one cub every nine years. Thus, the book can be used to illustrate the difference between the ratios of 9 to 1 and 1 to 9.

- *West Africa: Ghana, Ancient Japan,* and *Ancient Mexico* from the Ancient and Living Cultures series. GoodYearBooks, Scott Foresman, Glenview, IL, 1993.

This series of books contains designs from various cultures. Although stencils are included, we recommend that children use them only as examples since they are meant to be traced *around,* not *inside,* as in the activity.

Resources

- Appleton, Le Roy H. *American Indian Design and Decoration.* Dover Publications, New York, 1971.
- Sieber, Roy. *African Textiles and Decorative Arts.* The Museum of Modern Art, New York, 1972.
- Washburn, Dorothy D., and Donald W. Crowe. *Symmetries of Culture: Theory and Practice of Plane Pattern Analysis.* University of Washington Press, Seattle, 1988.
- Zaslavsky, Claudia. "Symmetry Along with Other Mathematical Concepts and Applications in African Life." In *Applications in School Mathematics* 1979 Yearbook, pp. 82–95. National Council of Teachers of Mathematics, Reston, VA, 1979.

At a Glance

Math Facts and Daily Practice and Problems

DPP Bits A and E provide practice with the subtraction facts in Groups 7 and 8. DPP Bit C encourages students to practice the subtraction facts in Group 7 using the *Subtraction Flash Cards.* Task B and Challenge D provide multidigit addition and subtraction practice. Task F develops strategies for the multiplication facts.

Part 1. Launching the Investigation
1. Read and discuss the *Stencilrama* Lab Pages in the Student Guide.
2. Students identify the two main variables, Number of Stencils (*N*) and Length of Border (*L*). *(Question 1)*
3. Students discuss *Questions 2–4.*

Part 2. Making a Stencil and Drawing the Picture
1. Make a stencil from an index card and model the procedure of making a border.
2. Each group chooses a design and cuts out a stencil.
3. Students draw a picture of the lab on the *Stencilrama* Lab Pages in the *Discovery Assignment Book.*

Part 3. Collecting and Recording the Data
1. Students use their stencils to begin their borders.
2. Students collect the data and record it on the *Stencilrama* Lab Pages in the *Discovery Assignment Book.*
3. Students look for patterns in the data table.
4. Observe students' abilities to collect and organize data.

Part 4. Graphing the Data
1. Student groups make decisions about labeling and scaling graphs and plotting the data.
2. Each student makes his or her individual graph.
3. Check that each graph has a title, the axes are scaled and labeled appropriately, the points are plotted correctly, and the line is drawn accurately. Observe students' abilities to graph and analyze data.

Part 5. Solving the Problems
1. Students use the data table and graph to answer *Questions 3–5* on the *Stencilrama* Lab Pages in the *Discovery Assignment Book,* using the three student rubrics to guide their work.
2. Students indicate on the graph how they used it to make predictions for *Questions 3–5.*
3. Help each group select an object to decorate with a border. Students then solve *Question 6.*

At a Glance

Homework

1. Assign Home Practice Parts 1 and 2.
2. Assign the word problems in Lesson 4.
3. Students study the subtraction facts in Groups 7 and 8 at home using the flash cards.

Assessment

1. Use the *Observational Assessment Record* to document students' abilities to measure length in inches and to collect, organize, graph, and analyze data.
2. Add this lab to students' portfolios.
3. Score *Questions 5* and *6* using the *TIMS Multidimensional Rubric*.

Connection

Read and discuss *Nine-In-One Grr! Grr!* by Blia Xiong or show the examples of stencils from *West Africa: Ghana, Ancient Japan,* and *Ancient Mexico* from the Ancient and Living Cultures series.

Answer key is on pages 41–44.

Notes:

Name _____   Date _____

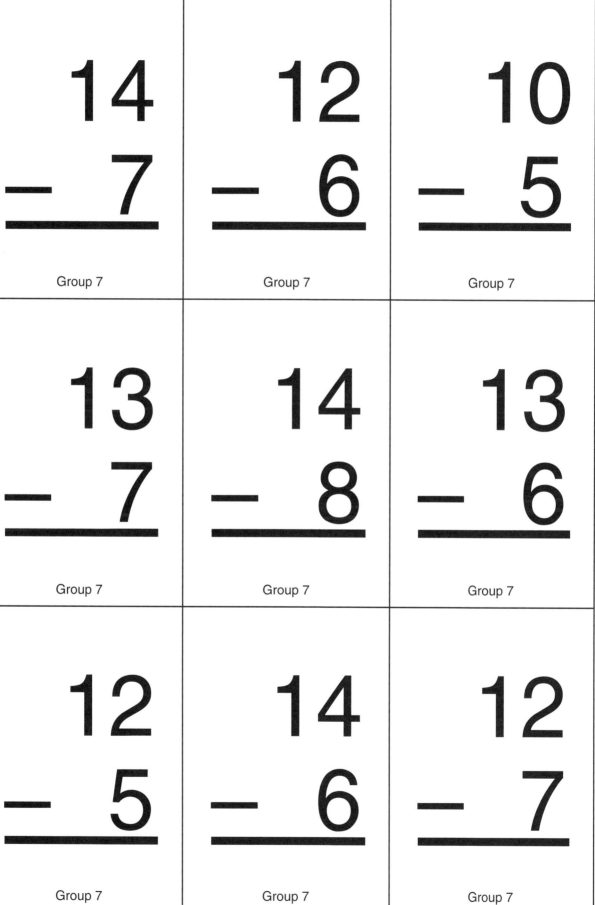

14 − 7 ―――― Group 7	12 − 6 ―――― Group 7	10 − 5 ―――― Group 7
13 − 7 ―――― Group 7	14 − 8 ―――― Group 7	13 − 6 ―――― Group 7
12 − 5 ―――― Group 7	14 − 6 ―――― Group 7	12 − 7 ―――― Group 7

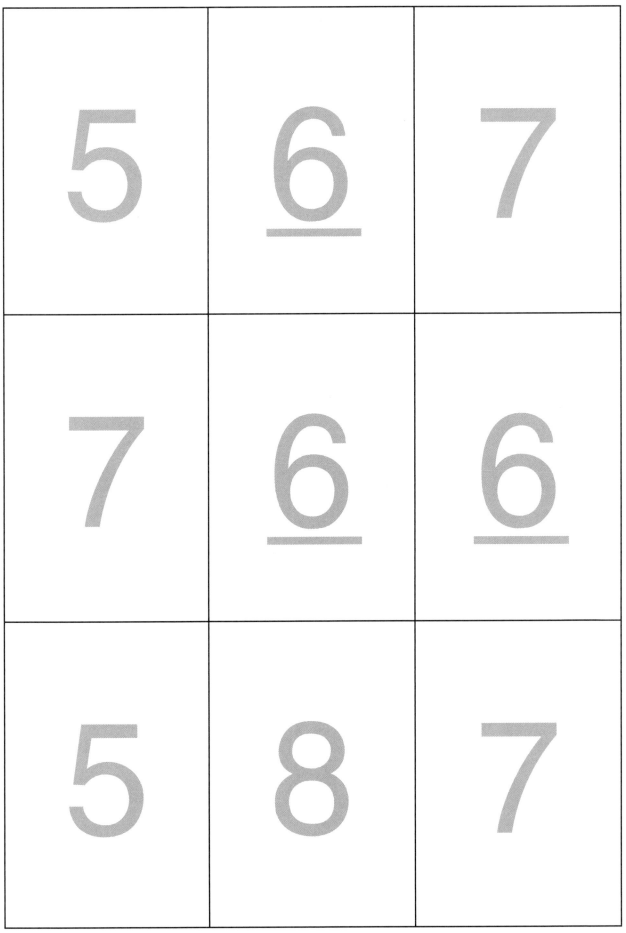

Subtraction Flash Cards: Group 7—Reverse Side

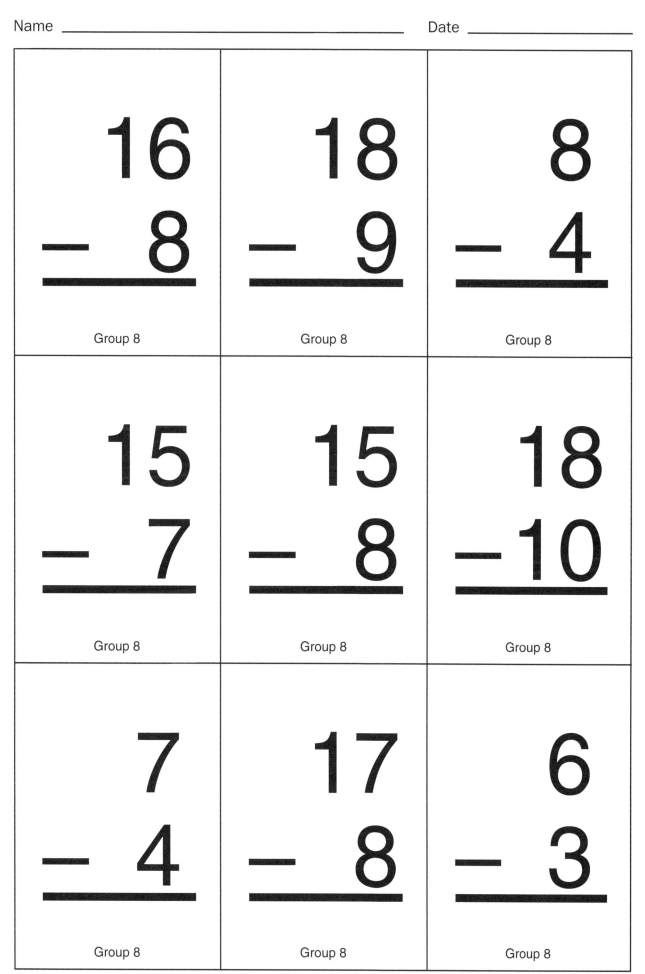

$$16 - 8$$

Group 8

$$18 - 9$$

Group 8

$$8 - 4$$

Group 8

$$15 - 7$$

Group 8

$$15 - 8$$

Group 8

$$18 - 10$$

Group 8

$$7 - 4$$

Group 8

$$17 - 8$$

Group 8

$$6 - 3$$

Group 8

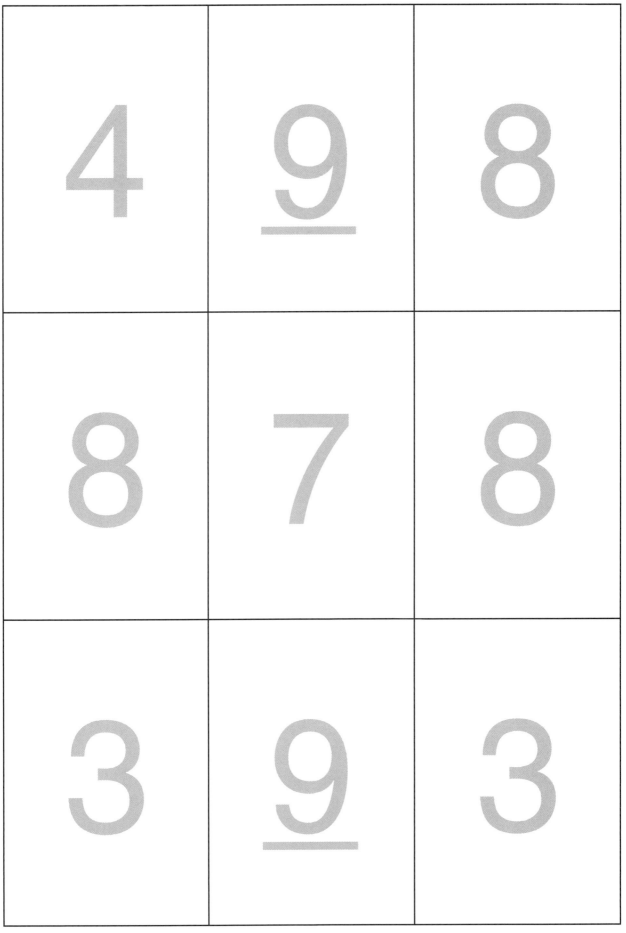

Subtraction Flash Cards: Group 8—Reverse Side

Student Guide (p. 132)

1. The main variables: Number of Stencils (*N*) and Length of Border (*L*).*

2. Size and shape of stencil must stay the same; no space between stencils; orientation of the cards (either vertical or horizontal) must be the same each time.*

3. They used the stencil four times and then measured the length of one, two, and four stencils.*

4. You need to measure the length of the board.*

So, the girls decided to make a graph of their stencil data. They used the graph to predict the number of stencils they needed for a border the length of Mrs. Cho's desk.

Let's say that your class decided to decorate your classroom using borders made with stencils. You would need to solve some problems. Here are some questions to discuss about Liz and Jody's data.

Discuss

1. What variables did Liz and Jody compare in their data table?

2. What stayed the same as they made their borders?

3. What did Liz and Jody do to collect the data they wrote in their data table?

4. Suppose Liz and Jody wanted to make a border across the top of the blackboard. What would they need to know to find the number of times they will use the stencil?

Some Designs from Cultures of the World

Below are designs found on objects from different cultures. Also included is one type of stencil you might make from the design.

1.

Design adapted from the Hmong People of Laos

Stencil adapted from design

Border made from stencil

132   SG • Grade 3 • Unit 10 • Lesson 1   Stencilrama

Student Guide - page 132

---

*Answers and/or discussion are included in the Lesson Guide.

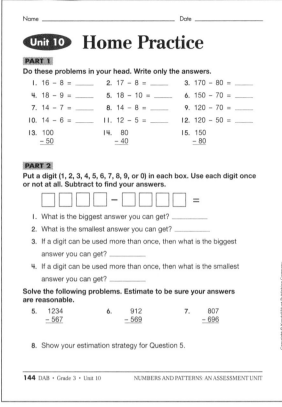

Discovery Assignment Book - page 144

Discovery Assignment Book - page 147

Discovery Assignment Book (p. 144)

Home Practice*

Part 1

1. 8	**2.** 9	**3.** 90
4. 9	**5.** 8	**6.** 80
7. 7	**8.** 6	**9.** 50
10. 8	**11.** 7	**12.** 70
13. 50	**14.** 40	**15.** 70

Part 2

1. 8853 (9876 − 1023)

2. 25; there are several ways to get this answer. One way is 4012 − 3987. There are many other combinations that give small differences (but not the smallest). For example, 2034 − 1987 = 47.

3. 9999 or 8999 (If leading 0 is allowed, 9999 − 0000 = 9999; if leading 0 is not allowed, 9999 − 1000 = 8999)

4. 0 (If leading 0 is allowed, 0000 − 0000 = 0; if leading 0 is not allowed, 1000 − 1000 = 0.)

5. 667

6. 343

7. 111

8. Possible strategy: 1200 − 600 = 600.

Discovery Assignment Book (p. 147)

Stencilrama†

1. Number of stencils (N) and Length of border (L)

2. Size and shape of stencil must stay the same; no space between stencils; orientation of the cards (either vertical or horizontal) must be the same each time.

*Answers for all the Home Practice in the *Discovery Assignment Book* are at the end of the unit.
†Answers and/or discussion are included in the Lesson Guide.

Discovery Assignment Book (pp. 148–149)

See the Lesson Guide for a sample picture, data table, and graph (Figures 4–6). Answers for *Questions 3–5* are based on the sample data in Figure 5.

3. **A.** 9 inches

  B. See the graph in Figure 6.

  C. Answers will vary. If students' answers do not match, there probably is a mistake in the graph. Students should be advised to correct their graphs or make new ones.

4. **A.** 21 inches. See the graph in Figure 6.

  B. You may find the length of seven by measuring seven stencils or by multiplying the length of one stencil by seven.

5. **A.** 12 stencils. See the graph in Figure 6.

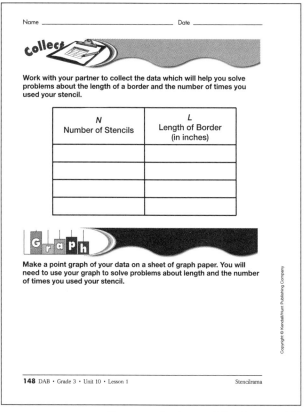

Discovery Assignment Book - page 148

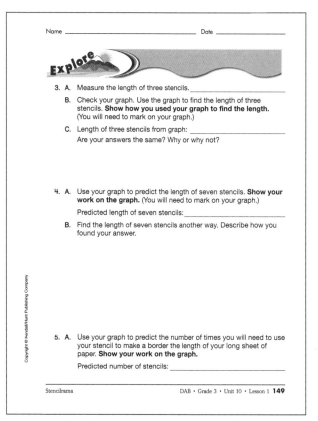

Discovery Assignment Book - page 149

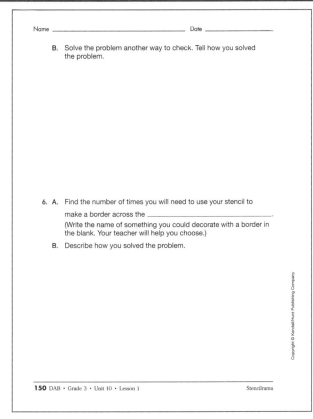

Discovery Assignment Book - page 150

Discovery Assignment Book (p. 150)

5. **B.** Some students may use their index cards while others write a multiplication or division sentence.

6. **A.** Objects chosen will vary.*

   B. Answers will vary.

*Answers and/or discussion are included in the Lesson Guide.

Lesson 2

Problem Game

Lesson Overview

Students review the subtraction facts by studying their *Subtraction Flash Cards* and then playing a review game. The game board is used several times in this curriculum with different card sets. Other games, introduced in previous units, are suggested for review as well.

Key Content

- Reviewing subtraction facts.

Math Facts

DPP Bit G asks students to practice the subtraction facts in Group 8 using *Subtraction Flash Cards*.

Homework

1. Remind students to study the subtraction facts using their flash cards.
2. Assign Home Practice Parts 3 and 4.

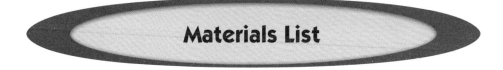

Materials List

Supplies and Copies

Student	Teacher
Supplies for Each Student • game token or centimeter connecting cube **Supplies for Each Student Group** • clear plastic spinner or pencil with paper clip	**Supplies**
Copies • 1 copy of *Subtraction Flash Cards: Groups 1–8* per student, copied back-to-back, optional (*Unit Resource Guide* Pages 37–40 and 51–62)	**Copies/Transparencies**

All blackline masters including assessment, transparency, and DPP masters are also on the Teacher Resource CD.

Student Books

Problem Game (*Student Guide* Page 135)
Problem Game Board (*Discovery Assignment Book* Page 151)
Problem Game Spinner (*Discovery Assignment Book* Page 153)

Daily Practice and Problems and Home Practice

DPP items G–H (*Unit Resource Guide* Page 16)
Home Practice Parts 3–4 (*Discovery Assignment Book* Page 145)

Note: Classrooms whose pacing differs significantly from the suggested pacing of the units should use the Math Facts Calendar in Section 4 of the *Facts Resource Guide* to ensure students receive the complete math facts program.

Daily Practice and Problems

Suggestions for using the DPPs are on page 49.

G. Bit: Subtraction Flash Cards: Group 8 (URG p. 16)

1. With a partner, sort the Flash Cards for Group 8 into three stacks: Facts I Know Quickly, Facts I Know Using a Strategy, and Facts I Need to Learn.

2. Update your *Subtraction Facts I Know* chart. Circle the facts you answered quickly. Underline those you know by using a strategy. Do nothing to those you still need to learn.

H. Task: Spot (URG p. 16)

Boo the Blob has a dog named Spot. Find Spot's area.

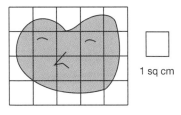

1 sq cm

TIMS Tip

If you do not have clear plastic spinners for the *Problem Game,* you can substitute a paper clip and pencil as shown in Unit 2 Lesson 2 *Spinning Sums.*

Teaching the Game

Remind students when they will take the quiz on the subtraction facts in Groups 7 and 8. This quiz is in Bit I in Lesson 3. Tell students they will be tested on all 72 subtraction facts. This test is in DPP Bit K. These facts are on their *Subtraction Facts I Know* charts and on *Subtraction Flash Cards: Groups 1–8.* The flash cards were distributed in the *Discovery Assignment Book* in Units 2–5 and are also available in this lesson.

Students can use the *Problem Game* to practice the subtraction facts. They play the game using the subtraction flash cards. You can assign certain groups of flash cards for each game students play. For example, review Groups 7 and 8 in the first game, Groups 1 and 2 in the second, and so on. Place the flash cards face up with the problems showing and the answers facing down.

Problem Game

Players

This is a game for two or more players.

Materials

- *Problem Game* game board
- *Subtraction Flash Cards for Groups 1–8*
- scratch paper for writing answers
- a clear spinner or a paper clip and a pencil
- a token for each player

Rules

1. Put the spinner over the spinner base on the *Problem Game Spinner* Game Page from the *Discovery Assignment Book.* (Or use a pencil and paper clip as a spinner.)
2. Put the flash cards, problem side up, on the Problem Cards rectangle.
3. Each player puts his or her token in the Start rectangle.
4. Spin to see who goes first.
5. When it is your turn, solve the top problem on the Problem Card stack. Say the answer aloud. If you are wrong, then your turn is over.
6. If you are right, spin the spinner, and move that many spaces.
7. Follow any directions written on the space you land on. Sometimes, arrows help you move forward or make you move back.
8. Put the Problem Card on the Discard rectangle.
9. The first player to reach the Finish rectangle (or beyond) is the winner.

This game can be used with different card sets. Your teacher will help you choose the type of problems you will solve each time you play.

Problem Game   SG • Grade 3 • Unit 10 • Lesson 2   135

Student Guide - page 135

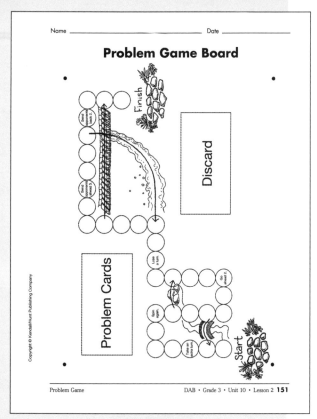

Discovery Assignment Book - page 151

Instructions for the *Problem Game* are on the *Problem Game* Game Page in the *Student Guide*. Students draw a card and solve the subtraction problem. If a player answers the problem correctly, he or she spins a spinner and advances his or her token on the *Problem Game Board* Game Page, which is in the *Discovery Assignment Book*. The first player to reach Finish is the winner.

Encourage students to study the subtraction facts by playing other games. The table below lists games students have played in previous units that can help them review the subtraction facts.

Games for Reviewing the Subtraction Facts

Game	Unit Number	Unit Name
Turn Over	1	Sampling and Classifying
Nine, Ten	2	Strategies: An Assessment Unit
Digits Game	6	More Adding and Subtracting
Tens Game	8	Mapping and Coordinates
Problem Game	10	Numbers and Patterns: An Assessment Unit

> **TIMS Tip**
>
> Students will use the *Problem Game Board* and *Problem Game Spinner* in Unit 11 Lesson 4. Make sure they keep these pages for future use.

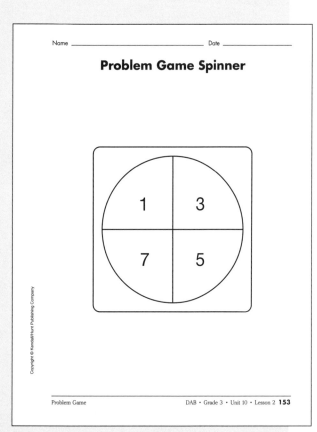

Discovery Assignment Book - page 153

Math Facts

- For DPP Bit G students practice subtraction facts using the *Subtraction Flash Cards* in Group 8.
- For Home Practice Part 3 students use multiplication facts to solve word problems.

Homework and Practice

- For DPP Task H students find the area of an irregular shape.
- For Home Practice Part 4 students solve word problems involving time.
- Students use the *Subtraction Flash Cards* to review for the quiz on the subtraction facts in Groups 7 and 8 in DPP item I in Lesson 3 and the inventory test on all eight groups in DPP item K of Lesson 3. Encourage students to concentrate on the facts not marked on their *Subtraction Facts I Know* charts.

Answers for Parts 3 and 4 of the Home Practice are in the Answer Key at the end of this lesson and at the end of this unit.

Name _____ Date _____

PART 3

1. Suppose we use the following standard masses to measure mass using a balance: 8-gram masses, 4-gram masses, and 1-gram masses. Think about how many of each you would need to use to balance a bottle of glue with a mass of 54 grams.
   A. How many of each would you need if you used the smallest number of masses possible?
   _____
   B. How many of each would you need if you used the largest number of masses possible?

2. Using the same standard masses, think about how many of each you would need to balance a note pad with a mass of 58 grams.
   A. How many of each would you need if you used the smallest number of masses possible?
   _____
   B. If you started with eight 4-gram masses, how many 8-gram and 1-gram masses would you still need to balance the note pad?
   _____

PART 4

1. Mr. Sosa teaches art class from 8:00 A.M. until 3:30 P.M. every Saturday. How many hours does he work on one Saturday?

2. How many hours will Mr. Sosa have worked after 4 Saturdays?

3. Last Saturday Mr. Sosa started art class at 8:00 A.M. He got sick and ended class $3\frac{1}{2}$ hours later. What time did he end the class?

NUMBERS AND PATTERNS: AN ASSESSMENT UNIT   DAB · Grade 3 · Unit 10 **145**

Discovery Assignment Book - page 145 (Answers on p. 63)

At a Glance

Math Facts and Daily Practice and Problems

DPP Bit G asks students to practice the subtraction facts in Group 8 using *Subtraction Flash Cards*. DPP Task H provides practice finding the area of an irregular shape.

Teaching the Game

1. Read the directions for *Problem Game* Game Page in the *Student Guide.*
2. Students practice their subtraction facts by playing the *Problem Game.*
3. Students review their subtraction facts by playing other games.

Homework

1. Remind students to study the subtraction facts using their flash cards.
2. Assign Home Practice Parts 3 and 4.

Answer Key is on page 63.

Notes:

12 − 9	12 − 10	13 − 9
Group 1	Group 1	Group 1
13 − 10	13 − 4	15 − 9
Group 1	Group 1	Group 1
15 − 10	15 − 6	19 − 10
Group 1	Group 1	Group 1

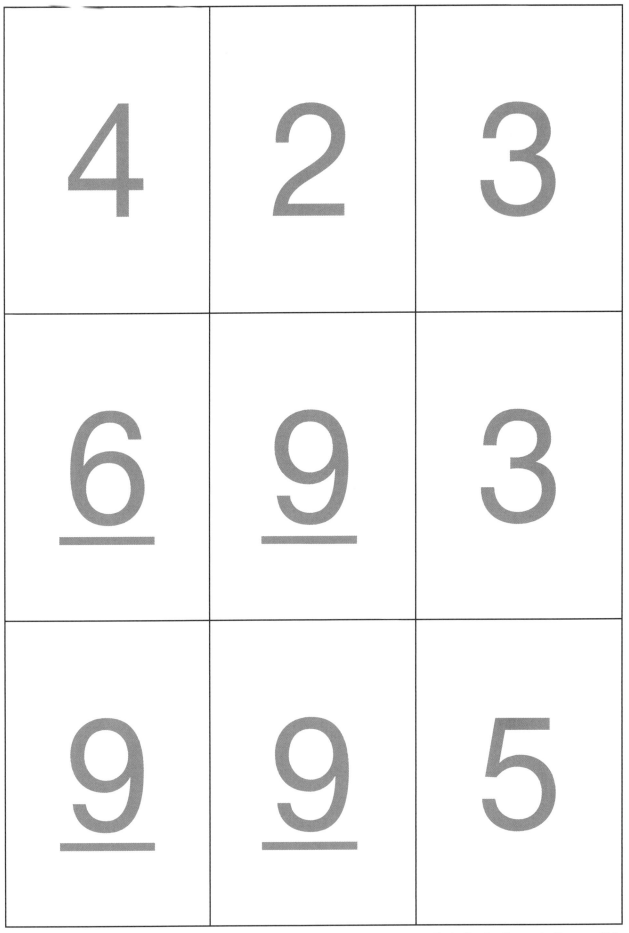

Subtraction Flash Cards: Group 1—Reverse Side

14 −10	14 − 9	14 − 5
Group 2	Group 2	Group 2
17 −10	17 − 9	11 − 9
Group 2	Group 2	Group 2
16 − 9	16 − 7	16 −10
Group 2	Group 2	Group 2

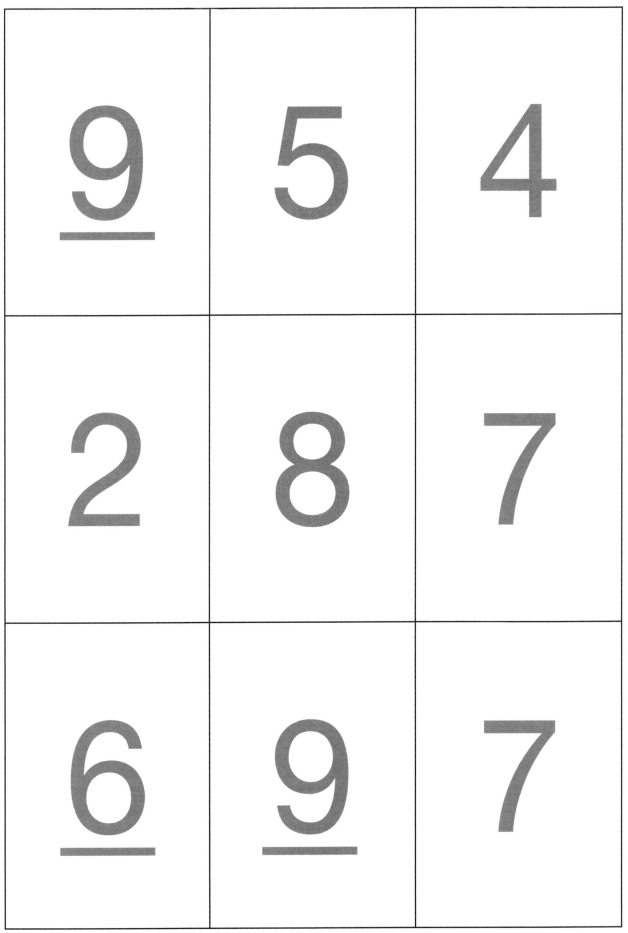

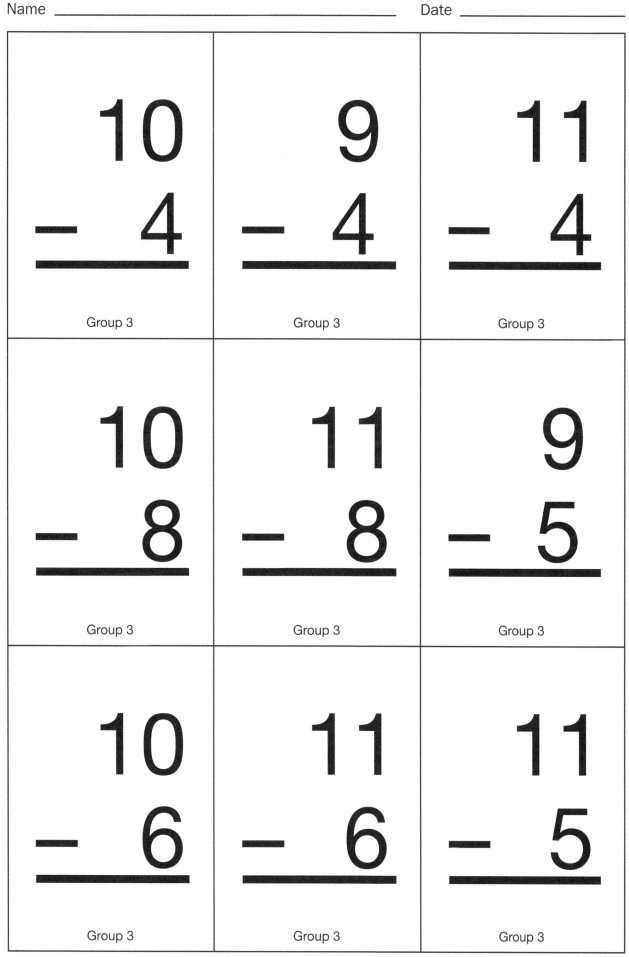

10 − 4 ——— Group 3	9 − 4 ——— Group 3	11 − 4 ——— Group 3
10 − 8 ——— Group 3	11 − 8 ——— Group 3	9 − 5 ——— Group 3
10 − 6 ——— Group 3	11 − 6 ——— Group 3	11 − 5 ——— Group 3

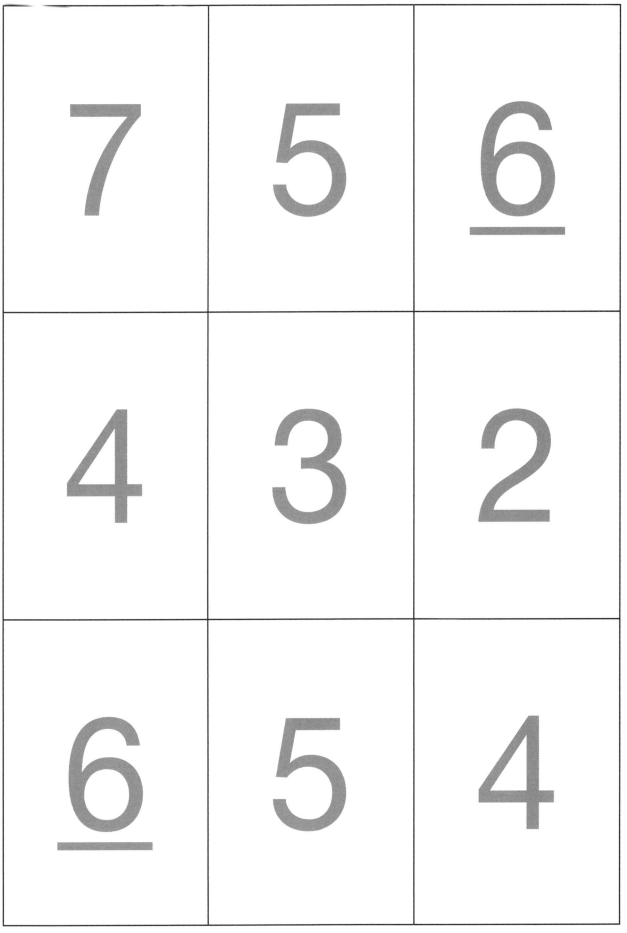

Subtraction Flash Cards: Group 3—Reverse Side

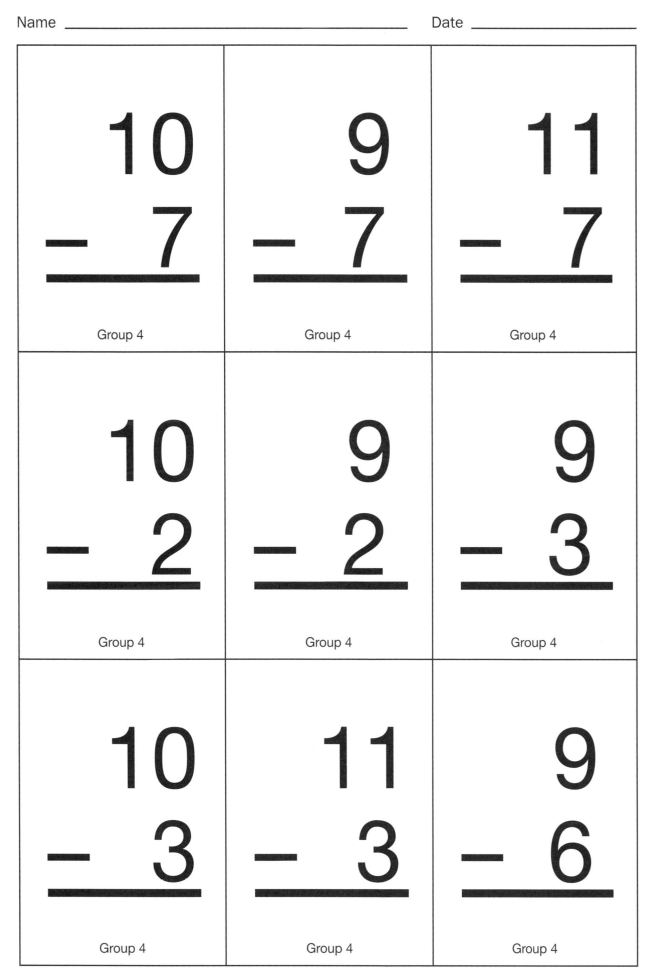

$$10 - 7$$

Group 4

$$9 - 7$$

Group 4

$$11 - 7$$

Group 4

$$10 - 2$$

Group 4

$$9 - 2$$

Group 4

$$9 - 3$$

Group 4

$$10 - 3$$

Group 4

$$11 - 3$$

Group 4

$$9 - 6$$

Group 4

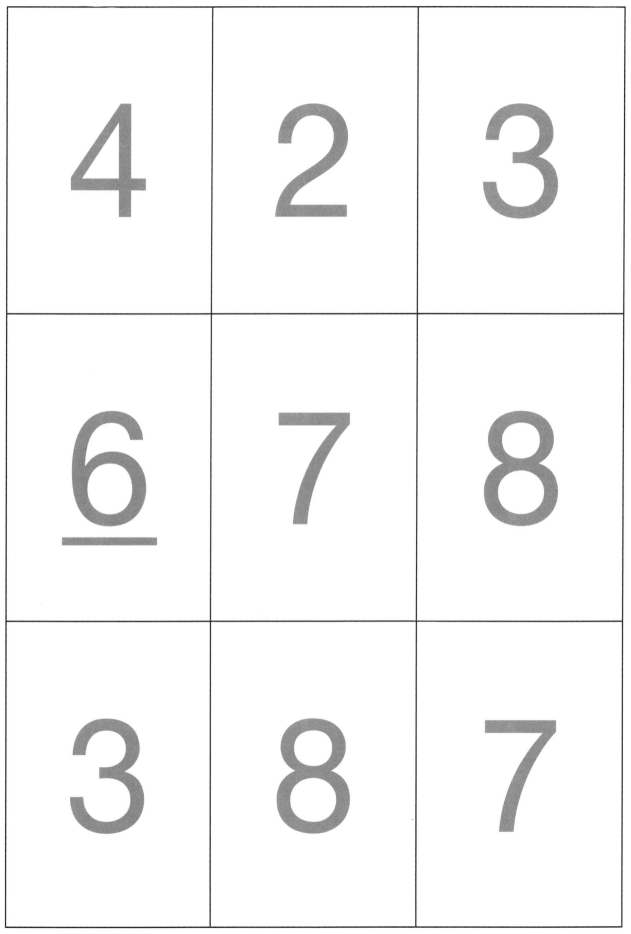

Subtraction Flash Cards: Group 4—Reverse Side

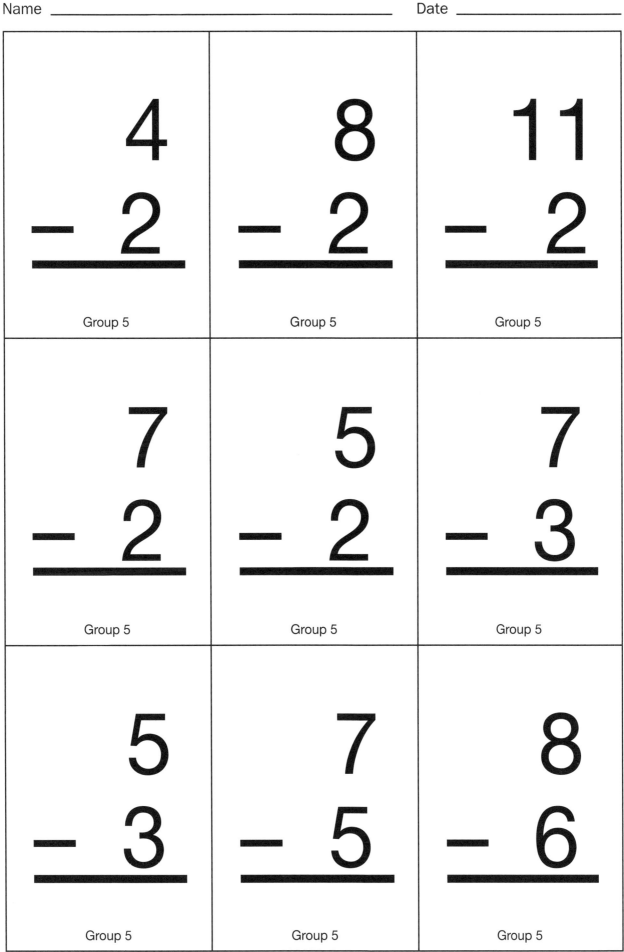

4 − 2	8 − 2	11 − 2
Group 5	Group 5	Group 5
7 − 2	5 − 2	7 − 3
Group 5	Group 5	Group 5
5 − 3	7 − 5	8 − 6
Group 5	Group 5	Group 5

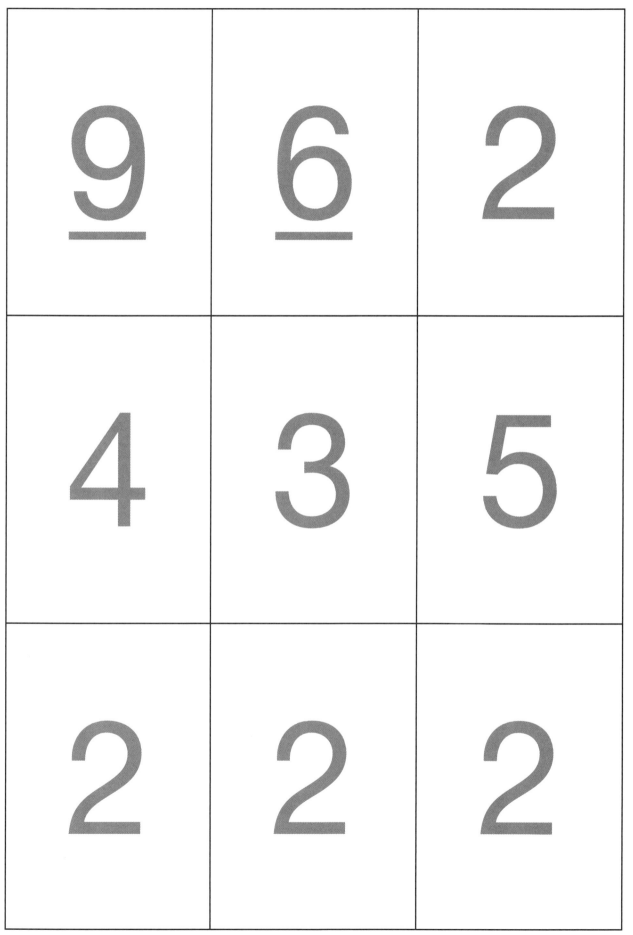

$\begin{array}{r} 12 \\ -\ 8 \\ \hline \end{array}$	$\begin{array}{r} 12 \\ -\ 4 \\ \hline \end{array}$	$\begin{array}{r} 13 \\ -\ 5 \\ \hline \end{array}$
Group 6	Group 6	Group 6
$\begin{array}{r} 13 \\ -\ 8 \\ \hline \end{array}$	$\begin{array}{r} 8 \\ -\ 5 \\ \hline \end{array}$	$\begin{array}{r} 8 \\ -\ 3 \\ \hline \end{array}$
Group 6	Group 6	Group 6
$\begin{array}{r} 6 \\ -\ 4 \\ \hline \end{array}$	$\begin{array}{r} 6 \\ -\ 2 \\ \hline \end{array}$	$\begin{array}{r} 12 \\ -\ 3 \\ \hline \end{array}$
Group 6	Group 6	Group 6

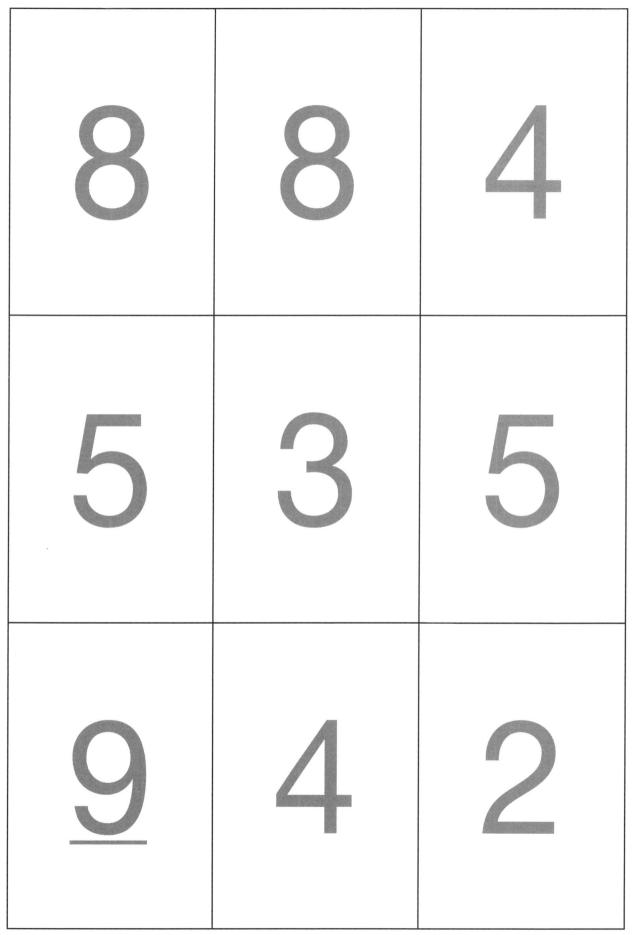

Subtraction Flash Cards: Group 6—Reverse Side

Discovery Assignment Book (p. 145)

Home Practice*

Part 3

1. **A.** Six 8-gram masses, one 4-gram mass, and two 1-gram masses

   B. fifty-four 1-gram masses

2. **A.** seven 8-gram masses and two 1-gram masses

   B. Possible response: three 8-gram masses and two 1-gram masses

Part 4

1. $7\frac{1}{2}$ hours

2. 30 hours

3. 11:30 A.M.

Name _____ Date _____

PART 3

1. Suppose we use the following standard masses to measure mass using a balance: 8-gram masses, 4-gram masses, and 1-gram masses. Think about how many of each you would need to use to balance a bottle of glue with a mass of 54 grams.

   A. How many of each would you need if you used the smallest number of masses possible?
   _____

   B. How many of each would you need if you used the largest number of masses possible?
   _____

2. Using the same standard masses, think about how many of each you would need to balance a note pad with a mass of 58 grams.

   A. How many of each would you need if you used the smallest number of masses possible?
   _____

   B. If you started with eight 4-gram masses, how many 8-gram and 1-gram masses would you still need to balance the note pad?
   _____

PART 4

1. Mr. Sosa teaches art class from 8:00 A.M. until 3:30 P.M. every Saturday. How many hours does he work on one Saturday?
   _____

2. How many hours will Mr. Sosa have worked after 4 Saturdays?
   _____

3. Last Saturday Mr. Sosa started art class at 8:00 A.M. He got sick and ended class $3\frac{1}{2}$ hours later. What time did he end the class?
   _____

NUMBERS AND PATTERNS: AN ASSESSMENT UNIT   DAB • Grade 3 • Unit 10 **145**

Discovery Assignment Book - page 145

---

*Answers for all the Home Practice in the *Discovery Assignment Book* are at the end of the unit.

Lesson 3

Class Party

Lesson Overview

Estimated Class Sessions

1-2

Student groups decide what they would serve at a class party given a list of party items and their prices, the number of students in the class, and a spending limit. Students explain their choices and show how their plans meet the given criteria.

Key Content

- Solving open-response problems.
- Communicating problem-solving strategies.
- Solving problems involving addition, subtraction, and multiplication.

Math Facts

DPP Bits I and K are assessments of the subtraction facts. DPP Tasks J and L develop strategies for the multiplication facts.

Homework

1. Assign the *Subtraction Flash Cards* to prepare for the *Subtraction Facts Inventory.*
2. Have students plan a party for the class.

Assessment

1. DPP Bit I assesses students' progress with the subtraction facts in Groups 7 and 8.
2. DPP Bit K assesses students' progress with all the subtraction facts.

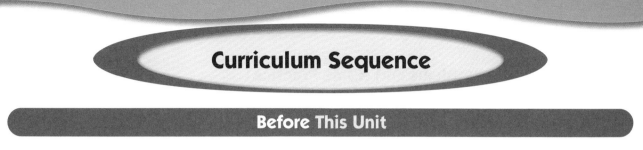

Curriculum Sequence

Before This Unit

Using Student Rubrics

Students used the Student Rubric: *Knowing* in Grade 3 Unit 2 Lesson 6 *Spinning Differences,* the Student Rubric: *Solving* in Unit 5 Lesson 5 *Joe the Goldfish,* and the Student Rubric: *Telling* in Unit 7 Lesson 2 *Katie's Job.* They used the rubrics as guides for writing about their solution strategies for open-response problems.

After This Unit

Using Student Rubrics

Students will continue to use the rubrics as they communicate their solution strategies. See Grade 3 Unit 20 Lesson 4 *Earning Money* for an example.

Materials List

Supplies and Copies

Student	Teacher
Supplies for Each Student • calculator	**Supplies**
Copies • 1 copy of *Subtraction Facts Quiz D* per student (*Unit Resource Guide* Page 20) • 1 copy of *Subtraction Facts Inventory* per student (*Unit Resource Guide* Page 21) • 1 copy of *Class Party* per student (*Unit Resource Guide* Page 73)	**Copies/Transparencies** • 1 transparency or poster of Student Rubrics: *Knowing, Solving,* and *Telling* (*Teacher Implementation Guide,* Assessment section)

All blackline masters including assessment, transparency, and DPP masters are also on the Teacher Resource CD.

Student Books

Student Rubrics. *Knowing, Solving,* and *Telling (Student Guide* Appendices A, B, and C and Inside Back Cover)

Daily Practice and Problems and Home Practice

DPP items I–L (*Unit Resource Guide* Pages 17–18)

Note: Classrooms whose pacing differs significantly from the suggested pacing of the units should use the Math Facts Calendar in Section 4 of the *Facts Resource Guide* to ensure students receive the complete math facts program.

Assessment Tools

TIMS Multidimensional Rubric (Teacher Implementation Guide, Assessment section)

Daily Practice and Problems

Suggestions for using the DPPs are on page 71.

I. Bit: Subtraction Facts Quiz D $\boxed{\frac{5}{\times 7}}$
(URG p. 17)

Students take *Subtraction Facts Quiz D,* which corresponds to *Subtraction Flash Cards: Groups 7* and *8.*

K. Bit: Subtraction Facts Inventory $\boxed{\frac{5}{\times 7}}$
(URG p. 18)

Students take an inventory test of the 72 subtraction facts that were studied in Groups 1–8 throughout Units 2–10.

J. Task: Moe and Joe Smart (URG p. 17) $\boxed{\frac{5}{\times 7}}$

1. Moe Smart is helping his brother Joe with his homework. Joe says, "Seven times eight is 54." How can Moe show Joe he is wrong?
2. Joe Smart says, "Six times eight is 46." How can Moe show Joe he is wrong?

L. Task: Double Doubles (URG p. 18) $\boxed{\frac{5}{\times 7}}$

1. $2 \times 6 =$	2. $2 \times 2 \times 6 =$
3. $4 \times 6 =$	4. $2 \times 7 =$
5. $2 \times 2 \times 7 =$	6. $4 \times 7 =$
7. $2 \times 8 =$	8. $2 \times 2 \times 8 =$
9. $4 \times 8 =$	10. $3 \times 7 =$
11. $2 \times 3 \times 7 =$	12. $6 \times 7 =$
13. $3 \times 8 =$	14. $2 \times 3 \times 8 =$
15. $6 \times 8 =$	

To begin the activity, read and discuss the directions on the *Class Party* Assessment Blackline Master. The problem is to plan a party for 25 students spending only $10.00 by choosing appropriate items from the given list. Emphasize that students must explain how they solved the problem and made their decisions. Students should work in groups of two or three. Each group can write an explanation of their solution and problem-solving process. Or, each student can write his or her own explanation after the group decides on a solution.

Give students an opportunity to make revisions based on your comments before assigning final grades for the papers. Your comments might include a reminder that each number should be clearly labeled (such as three pitchers of lemonade or two packages of cookies) or include a request for a more detailed explanation of how the group made their decisions.

Review the Student Rubrics: *Knowing, Solving,* and *Telling* with students. In the following discussion, you will find three examples of student work along with scores for each dimension based on the following questions.

Knowing

- Did students choose appropriate operations? The students' solutions may involve the following operations:

  Multiplication or repeated addition to find the total expenditure of an item for the whole class;

  Multidigit addition of these subtotals to find the total expenditure; and

  Subtraction to compare the subtotal with $10.00 and addition if other items are then added to the old total.

- Did students compute accurately?

Solving

- Does students' work demonstrate a strategy for trying out plans and choosing the best plan for the party?

- Did students organize their work?

- Did students look back at the problem and draw appropriate conclusions?

- Did students use any relevant outside information?

> ### TIMS Tip
>
> Students may write a given number of cents incorrectly by using a decimal point and the cents sign (¢) simultaneously. For example, Manuel wrote ".90¢" instead of "90¢" or "$.90." Later, he wrote ".2¢" for "$.02," incorrectly placing the decimal point. You may want to review the way to write cents before students begin working on the problem.

- Did students clearly describe how they solved problems?

- Did students use correct number sentences or other symbolic representations?

- Did students tell how or why they made decisions? This could mean showing all the plans that the group tried and indicating which plans worked, which plans did not, and why.

The samples of student work presented in Figures 7–9 show varying levels of content knowledge, problem-solving abilities, and communication skills. The following scores reflect ratings according to the *TIMS Multidimensional Rubric*.

Scores for Manuel, Phillip, and Marina

Knowing, 2

Manuel, Phillip, and Marina made many calculations on their practice sheet as they tried out various plans for their party. In this way, they showed an understanding of when and how to use the four operations. However, they made errors in some of their calculations involving multidigit addition.

Solving, 4

These students organized their work in a logical fashion, which demonstrated they had devised an effective strategy for testing several plans. They reviewed these plans, evaluated them, and made decisions accordingly.

Telling, 3

This group's work reveals a clear picture of their problem-solving process. They listed the items for four different plans and labeled each item in the plan. However, they did not show number sentences for subtotals, such as $3 \times \$2.50 = \$7.50$, for lemonade. They gave a reason for accepting or rejecting the plan. For example, on Plan 4 they wrote, "Does not work! too high." Marina, Manuel, and Phillip wrote a paragraph explaining the plan they chose, but the paragraph did not include their decision-making process. The plan they chose used the least amount of money, so they added an item to the list of possible items: a piñata. Although 90¢ is not reasonable for a piñata, they did communicate their reasoning for this addition.

Practice sheet

1. Lemonade $7.50
   Cups $1.38
   napkins 49¢
   popcorn $1.09
   all together $10.46

   second most money spent

2. icecream bars $7.50
   cookies $1.98
   napkins 49¢
   all together $9.97

   most money spent

3. icecream bars $7.50
   popcorn $1.09
   napkins .49
   all together $9.98¢

   included mine pinyata all ready added to amount

   we chose this one

   less money spent

4. lemonde $7.50
   cups $1.38
   cookies 1.98
   $10.86

   does! not! work!   *too high*

We spend the money on, icecream bars, popcorn, napkins, that makes $9.08. We have .92¢ left, so we make our owen. It is a miney pinata, it costs .90¢ (150 pices of candy incude, that makes it so each kid would get 6 candys.) left over, .2¢

Figure 7: *Practice sheet used by Manuel, Phillip, and Marina*

Scores for Tanya and Li

Knowing, 4

Tanya and Li showed that they had a very good understanding of how to use the operations to solve the problem. All their computations were accurate, including finding the cost of $2\frac{1}{2}$ pitchers.

Solving, 2

This group's work shows they were looking for a plan that would provide a drink for all 25 students at a low cost by making $2\frac{1}{2}$ pitchers of lemonade, serving popcorn, and buying cups and napkins. However, since their solution leaves them with $1.48, they did not follow the direction to "use as much of the $10.00 as you can." This is an important element of the problem not incorporated into their plan. Li and Tanya did not show that they tried any other options to resolve this problem.

Telling, 3

Li and Tanya used number sentences with the cost of each item clearly labeled to show the steps they followed to solve the problem. They did not indicate, however, how they made their decisions.

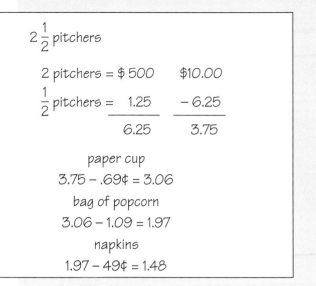

Figure 8: *Tanya and Li's work*

Item	Cost
pitcher of lemonade (10 servings)	$2.50
paper cups (package of 24)	69¢
ice cream bars	30¢
oatmeal cookies (package of 16)	99¢
bag of popcorn (30 servings)	$1.09
napkins (package of 50)	49¢

$8.91 ¢

7.50 $

Total
6.06

1 bag of popcorn
$8.91 + $1.09
$1.41 left!
.98¢ napkins
43¢ Left over

Figure 9: *Martin and Kate's work*

Journal Prompt

Describe how your group worked together to plan the party. Did your group cooperate to find the solution? Did each member have a job? How did you settle your disagreements?

Scores for Martin and Kate

Knowing, 4

Kate and Martin applied the appropriate operations to the problem and accurately computed the cost of the items they chose for the party: 25 ice cream bars for $7.50, one bag of popcorn for $1.09, and two packages of napkins for $.98. They correctly found that they would have 43¢ left over.

Solving, 1

These students did not show any systematic attempt to explore other possible plans or organize their work in an effective manner. They gave no evidence that they looked back at their solution or reflected on their work in any way.

Telling, 2

Although this group labeled each step, they did not use number sentences systematically, and it is very difficult to follow their thinking. They did not tell us how they solved the problem, if they tried any other plans for the party, or how they chose this one.

Tasks J and L develop strategies for the multiplication facts for the last six facts.

Homework and Practice

- Challenge students to plan a party for the class. They can choose the items they wish to serve and find the cost of those items at a grocery store. Give them a limit on the amount of money they can spend and ask them to write a clear explanation of their plans for the party.
- Assign *Subtraction Flash Cards* to review every night for homework in preparation for the inventory test.

Assessment

- DPP Bit I is a quiz on the subtraction facts in Groups 7 and 8.
- DPP Bit K is a test on all the subtraction facts.
- Add the *Class Party* activity to students' portfolios so you can compare students' work on this activity to their work on *Joe the Goldfish* (Unit 5), *Katie's Job* (Unit 7), other assessment pages in previous units, as well as similar activities in the future.

At a Glance

Math Facts and Daily Practice and Problems

DPP Bits I and K are assessments of the subtraction facts. DPP Tasks J and L develop strategies for the multiplication facts.

Teaching the Activity

1. Students read and discuss the directions on the *Class Party* Assessment Blackline Master.
2. Emphasize that students must explain how they solved the problem and made their decisions.
3. Review one or more of the Student Rubrics: *Knowing, Solving,* and *Telling.*
4. Students work in groups to solve the problem and write the explanation.
5. Review first drafts of student work.
6. Students make revisions based on teacher's comments.

Homework

1. Assign the *Subtraction Flash Cards* to prepare for the *Subtraction Facts Inventory.*
2. For homework, have students plan a party for the class.

Assessment

1. DPP Bit I assesses students' progress with the subtraction facts in Groups 7 and 8.
2. DPP Bit K assesses students' progress with all the subtraction facts.
3. Score students' work on the *Class Party* problem using the *TIMS Multidimensional Rubric.* Add students' work to their portfolios.

Answer Key is on page 74.

Notes:

Class Party

Suppose there are 25 students in your class and you have $10 for a class party. Use the prices in the table to plan a party.

Tell how you would spend the money, and explain why you would spend it that way. Use as much of the $10 as you can, but do not plan to spend more than $10. (There is no tax.) Be sure your plan works for a class of 25.

Write your plan on another piece of paper. Be sure to explain how you solved the problem and how you made your decisions.

Item	Cost
pitcher of lemonade (10 servings)	$2.50
paper cups (package of 24)	69¢
ice cream bars	30¢
oatmeal cookies (package of 16)	99¢
bag of popcorn (30 servings)	$1.09
napkins (package of 50)	49¢

Name _____ Date _____

Class Party

Suppose there are 25 students in your class and you have $10 for a class party. Use the prices in the table to plan a party.

Tell how you would spend the money, and explain why you would spend it that way. Use as much of the $10 as you can, but do not plan to spend more than $10. (There is no tax.) Be sure your plan works for a class of 25.

Write your plan on another piece of paper. Be sure to explain how you solved the problem and how you made your decisions.

Item	Cost
pitcher of lemonade (10 servings)	$2.50
paper cups (package of 24)	69¢
ice cream bars	30¢
oatmeal cookies (package of 16)	99¢
bag of popcorn (30 servings)	$1.09
napkins (package of 50)	49¢

Assessment Blackline Master   URG • Grade 3 • Unit 10 • Lesson 3   73

Unit Resource Guide - page 73

Class Party

See Lesson Guide 3 (Figures 7–9) for samples of student work.*

*Answers and/or discussion are included in the Lesson Guide.

Optional Lesson 4

Word Problems for Review

Estimated Class Sessions

1

Students solve a set of word problems to review for the midyear test.

Key Content

- Solving multistep word problems.
- Communicating solutions.

Homework

Assign some or all of the problems for homework.

Materials List

Supplies and Copies

Student	Teacher
Supplies for Each Student • ruler	**Supplies**
Copies	**Copies/Transparencies**

All blackline masters including assessment, transparency, and DPP masters are also on the Teacher Resource CD.

Student Books

Word Problems for Review (*Student Guide* Pages 136–137)

Teaching the Activity

Students can work on these problems individually, in pairs, or in groups. Students may complete them all at once or you can distribute them throughout the unit. Create additional problems as needed or encourage students to write their own.

Homework and Practice

Assign some or all of the problems for homework.

Extension

Ask students to write and illustrate their own problems involving changing money either at a bookstore or a different type of store. Have students swap problems with a partner. After students solve their partners' problems, they can check each other's solutions and strategies.

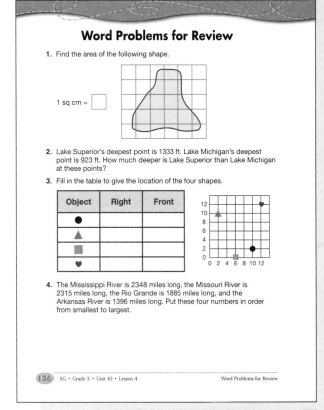

Word Problems for Review

1. Find the area of the following shape.

   1 sq cm = ☐

2. Lake Superior's deepest point is 1333 ft. Lake Michigan's deepest point is 923 ft. How much deeper is Lake Superior than Lake Michigan at these points?

3. Fill in the table to give the location of the four shapes.

Object	Right	Front
●		
▲		
▣		
♥		

4. The Mississippi River is 2348 miles long, the Missouri River is 2315 miles long, the Rio Grande is 1885 miles long, and the Arkansas River is 1396 miles long. Put these four numbers in order from smallest to largest.

Student Guide - page 136 (Answers on p. 79)

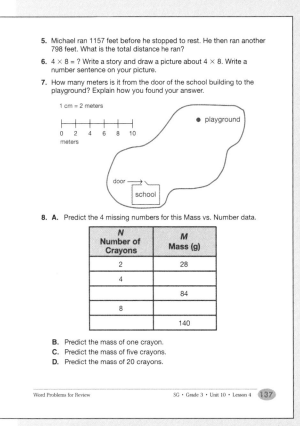

5. Michael ran 1157 feet before he stopped to rest. He then ran another 798 feet. What is the total distance he ran?

6. $4 \times 8 = ?$ Write a story and draw a picture about 4×8. Write a number sentence on your picture.

7. How many meters is it from the door of the school building to the playground? Explain how you found your answer.

   1 cm = 2 meters

   0 2 4 6 8 10
   meters

   ● playground

   door ⟶

   school

8. **A.** Predict the 4 missing numbers for this Mass vs. Number data.

N Number of Crayons	M Mass (g)
2	28
4	
	84
8	
	140

   B. Predict the mass of one crayon.
   C. Predict the mass of five crayons.
   D. Predict the mass of 20 crayons.

Student Guide - page 137 (Answers on p. 79)

At a Glance

Teaching the Activity

1. Students solve the problems on the *Word Problems for Review* Activity Pages in the *Student Guide.*
2. Students discuss their solution strategies with the class.

Homework

Assign some or all of the problems for homework.

Extension

Have students write and illustrate problems involving changing money at the store. Students can then swap the problems to solve.

Answer Key is on page 79.

Notes:

Student Guide (p. 136)

Word Problems for Review

I. 12–14 sq cm

2. Lake Superior's deepest point is 410 feet deeper than Lake Michigan's.

3.

Object	Right	Front
●	10	2
▲	2	10
■	6	0
♥	12	12

4. 1396, 1885, 2315, 2348

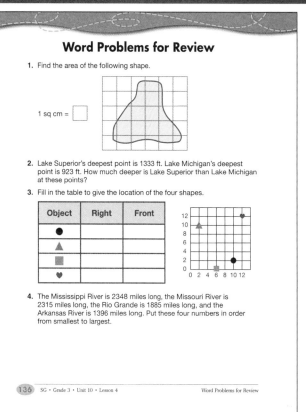

Word Problems for Review

1. Find the area of the following shape.

    1 sq cm = ☐

2. Lake Superior's deepest point is 1333 ft. Lake Michigan's deepest point is 923 ft. How much deeper is Lake Superior than Lake Michigan at these points?

3. Fill in the table to give the location of the four shapes.

Object	Right	Front
●		
▲		
■		
♥		

4. The Mississippi River is 2348 miles long, the Missouri River is 2315 miles long, the Rio Grande is 1885 miles long, and the Arkansas River is 1396 miles long. Put these four numbers in order from smallest to largest.

136   SG • Grade 3 • Unit 10 • Lesson 4   Word Problems for Review

Student Guide - page 136

Student Guide (p. 137)

5. 1955 feet

6. $4 \times 8 = 32$; stories and pictures will vary.

7. 12 meters: Students can measure the distance from school to the playground with a ruler. The distance is 6 cm. Using the scale $2 \times 6 = 12$ m

8. A.

N	M (in grams)
2	28
4	56
6	84
8	112
10	140

B. 14 g   **C.** 70 g   **D.** 280 g

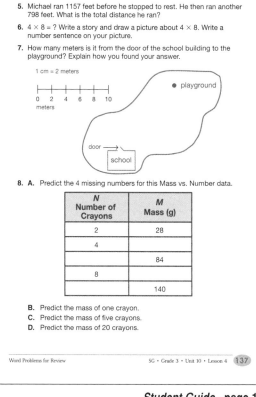

5. Michael ran 1157 feet before he stopped to rest. He then ran another 798 feet. What is the total distance he ran?

6. $4 \times 8 = ?$ Write a story and draw a picture about 4×8. Write a number sentence on your picture.

7. How many meters is it from the door of the school building to the playground? Explain how you found your answer.

    1 cm = 2 meters

    • playground
    door →
    school

8. A. Predict the 4 missing numbers for this Mass vs. Number data.

N Number of Crayons	M Mass (g)
2	28
4	
	84
8	
	140

    B. Predict the mass of one crayon.
    C. Predict the mass of five crayons.
    D. Predict the mass of 20 crayons.

Word Problems for Review   SG • Grade 3 • Unit 10 • Lesson 4   137

Student Guide - page 137

Lesson 5

Midyear Test

Lesson Overview

Estimated Class Sessions

1

Students take a paper-and-pencil test consisting of 10 short items. These items test skills and concepts studied in the first nine units.

Key Content

- Assessing the concepts studied in Units 1 through 9.

Assessment

1. Add students' tests to their portfolios.
2. Transfer documentation from the Unit 10 *Observational Assessment Record* to students' *Individual Assessment Record Sheets.*

Materials List

Supplies and Copies

Student	Teacher
Supplies for Each Student • calculator • ruler	**Supplies**
Copies • 1 copy of *Midyear Test* per student (*Unit Resource Guide* Pages 84–90)	**Copies/Transparencies**

All blackline masters including assessment, transparency, and DPP masters are also on the Teacher Resource CD.

Daily Practice and Problems and Home Practice

DPP items M–N (*Unit Resource Guide* Page 19)

Note: Classrooms whose pacing differs significantly from the suggested pacing of the units should use the Math Facts Calendar in Section 4 of the *Facts Resource Guide* to ensure students receive the complete math facts program.

Assessment Tools

Observational Assessment Record (*Unit Resource Guide* Pages 9–10)
Individual Assessment Record Sheet (*Teacher Implementation Guide,* Assessment section)

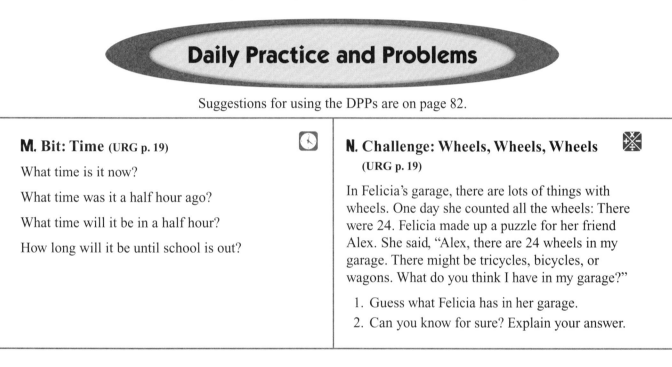

Daily Practice and Problems

Suggestions for using the DPPs are on page 82.

M. Bit: Time (URG p. 19)

What time is it now?

What time was it a half hour ago?

What time will it be in a half hour?

How long will it be until school is out?

N. Challenge: Wheels, Wheels, Wheels (URG p. 19)

In Felicia's garage, there are lots of things with wheels. One day she counted all the wheels: There were 24. Felicia made up a puzzle for her friend Alex. She said, "Alex, there are 24 wheels in my garage. There might be tricycles, bicycles, or wagons. What do you think I have in my garage?"

1. Guess what Felicia has in her garage.
2. Can you know for sure? Explain your answer.

Teaching the Activity

Students take the test individually. Although it was designed for just one class session, you may want to give students more time to complete it. Each student will need a ruler and should have access to a calculator for the second part of the test.

The first part *(Questions 1–7)* consists of addition and subtraction problems; they are included in the test to assess students' fluency with multidigit addition and subtraction. Students should complete these items without using a calculator. However, the problems may be solved using more than one strategy. Once students complete these items, they should have the option of using a calculator for the remaining problems.

Ask students to follow the directions for each item. Some ask them to tell how they solved the problem. Encourage students to give full explanations for the problem-solving process used.

The problems on this test cover a wide variety of skills and concepts. If you have skipped lessons, you may choose not to use certain test items.

Homework and Practice

DPP Bit M provides practice telling time. Challenge N is a problem with multiple solutions.

Assessment

- Add this completed test to your students' portfolios so you can compare their performance on it to their performance on similar activities in the future.
- Transfer appropriate assessment information from the Unit 10 *Observational Assessment Record* to students' *Individual Assessment Record Sheets*.

At a Glance

Math Facts and Daily Practice and Problems

DPP Bit M practices telling time. Challenge N is a word problem.

Teaching the Activity

1. Students complete the first part *(Questions 1–7)* of the *Midyear Test* without a calculator.
2. Students complete the remaining items with a calculator and a ruler available.

Assessment

1. Add students' completed tests to their portfolios.
2. Transfer documentation from the Unit 10 *Observational Assessment Record* to students' *Individual Assessment Record Sheets.*

Answer Key is on pages 91–93.

Notes:

Midyear Test

You may *not* use your calculator on Part 1. You may use your calculator for Part 2.

Part 1

1. In an average year it rains 48 days in El Paso, Texas, and 137 days in Columbus, Ohio. How many more days does it rain in Columbus than in El Paso? Show how you found your answer.

2. A computer costs $1166, and a printer costs $849. What is the total cost of the computer and printer? Show how you found your answer.

Solve each problem. Estimate to be sure your answer is reasonable.

3. $\begin{array}{r} 2436 \\ +6579 \\ \hline \end{array}$

4. $\begin{array}{r} 4321 \\ -1789 \\ \hline \end{array}$

5. $\begin{array}{r} 502 \\ -198 \\ \hline \end{array}$

6. Explain your estimation strategy for Question 3.

7. Explain how to solve Question 5 using mental math.

For the rest of the test, you may use any tools you used in class. For example, you may use a ruler or a calculator.

Part 2

8. All the students in Kim's class did pull-ups in gym. Here is the table that shows how many they did. Make a bar graph of the data on the following piece of graph paper.

Number of Pull-ups	Number of Students
0	10
1	3
2	3
3	4
4	2
5	0
6	1

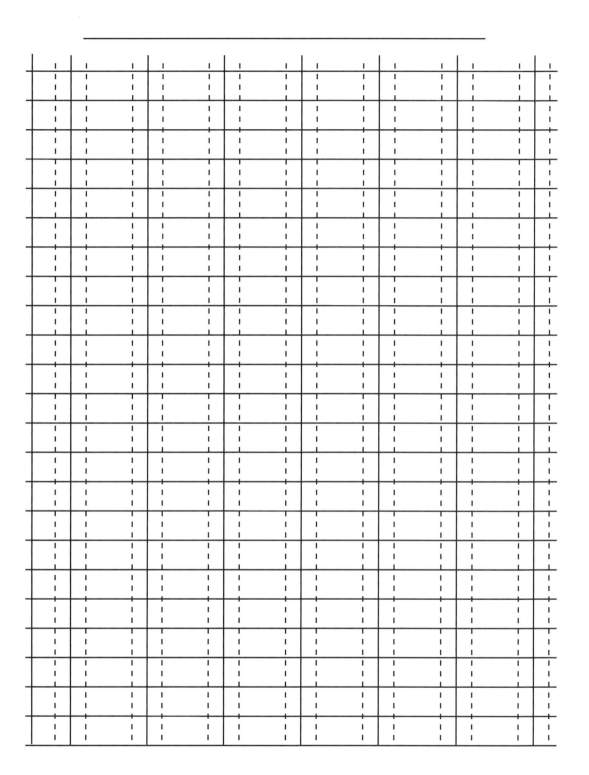

9. A. What was the greatest number of pull-ups any student could do?

    B. What was the most common number of pull-ups?

10. $6 \times 4 = ?$ Write a story and draw a picture about 6×4. Write a complete number sentence on your picture.

11. A. The largest swordfish ever caught weighed 1182 pounds. The largest hammerhead shark ever caught weighed 991 pounds. The largest Greenland shark ever caught weighed 1709 pounds. Put these numbers in order from smallest to largest.

_____   _____   _____
smallest   *largest*

B. Show 1709 using base-ten shorthand.

12. Find the area of the following shape:

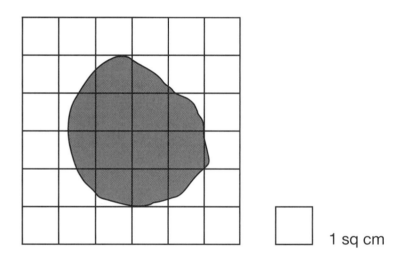

1 sq cm

Area:

13. Draw the shapes at the correct locations.

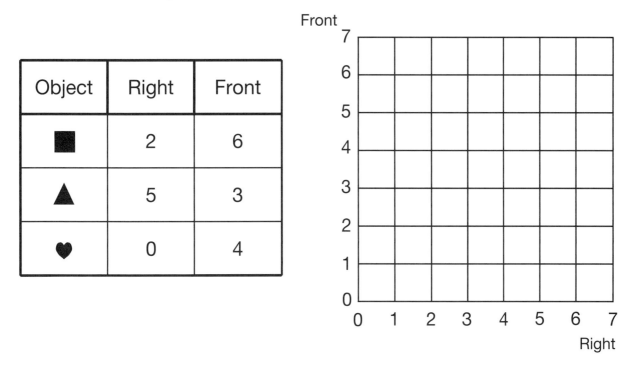

Object	Right	Front
■	2	6
▲	5	3
♥	0	4

14. How many miles is it from the Pirate's Cave to the treasure? _____
Show how you found your answer.

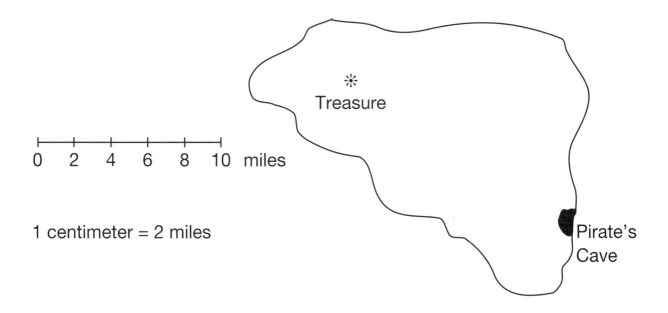

1 centimeter = 2 miles

15. Rosa is selling candy for her soccer team. Use the graph to answer
   the questions.

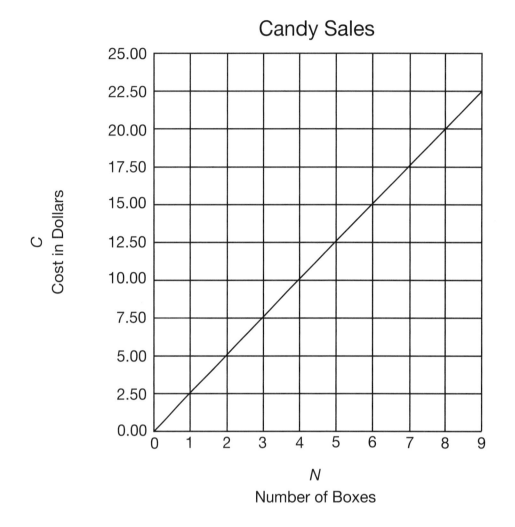

A. How much does one box of candy cost?

B. How much do seven boxes of candy cost? Mark on your graph
   to show how you found your answer.

Unit Resource Guide (p. 84)

Midyear Test

1. 89 days
2. $2,015
3. 9015
4. 2532
5. 304
6. Possible strategy: $2500 + 6500 = 9000$
7. Possible strategy: Count up 2 to 200, 300 from 200 to 500, and then 2 more to 502: $2 + 300 + 2 = 304$.

Name _____ Date _____

Midyear Test

You may *not* use your calculator on Part 1. You may use your calculator for Part 2.

Part 1

1. In an average year it rains 48 days in El Paso, Texas, and 137 days in Columbus, Ohio. How many more days does it rain in Columbus than in El Paso? Show how you found your answer.

2. A computer costs $1166, and a printer costs $849. What is the total cost of the computer and printer? Show how you found your answer.

Solve each problem. Estimate to be sure your answer is reasonable.

3. 2436
   +6579

4. 4321
   −1789

5. 502
   −198

6. Explain your estimation strategy for Question 3.

7. Explain how to solve Question 5 using mental math.

Unit Resource Guide - page 84

Unit Resource Guide (p. 85)

8.

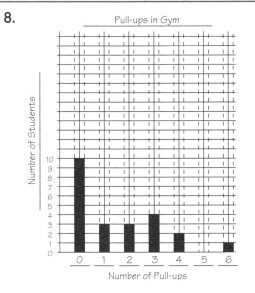

Pull-ups in Gym

Name _____ Date _____

For the rest of the test, you may use any tools you used in class. For example, you may use a ruler or a calculator.

Part 2

8. All the students in Kim's class did pull-ups in gym. Here is the table that shows how many they did. Make a bar graph of the data on the following piece of graph paper.

Number of Pull-ups	Number of Students
0	10
1	3
2	3
3	4
4	2
5	0
6	1

Unit Resource Guide - page 85

Name _____ Date _____

9. A. What was the greatest number of pull-ups any student could do?

B. What was the most common number of pull-ups?

10. 6 × 4 = ? Write a story and draw a picture about 6 × 4. Write a complete number sentence on your picture.

Copyright © Kendall/Hunt Publishing Company

Assessment Blackline Master   URG • Grade 3 • Unit 10 • Lesson 5   **87**

Unit Resource Guide - page 87

Unit Resource Guide (p. 87)

9. A. six pull-ups

B. None or 0 pull-ups

10. 24; stories and pictures will vary.

Name _____ Date _____

11. A. The largest swordfish ever caught weighed 1182 pounds. The largest hammerhead shark ever caught weighed 991 pounds. The largest Greenland shark ever caught weighed 1709 pounds. Put these numbers in order from smallest to largest.

_____   _____   _____
   smallest   *largest*

B. Show 1709 using base-ten shorthand.

12. Find the area of the following shape:

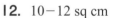

1 sq cm

Area:

Copyright © Kendall/Hunt Publishing Company

88   URG • Grade 3 • Unit 10 • Lesson 5   Assessment Blackline Master

Unit Resource Guide - page 88

Unit Resource Guide (p. 88)

11. A. 991 pounds, 1182 pounds, 1709 pounds

B. ▱ ▱▱▱▱▱ ||||| ▱▱ ||||

12. 10−12 sq cm

Unit Resource Guide (p. 89)

13.

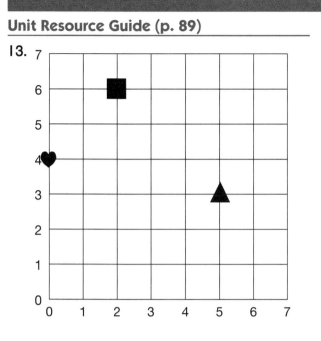

14. 7 cm = 14 miles

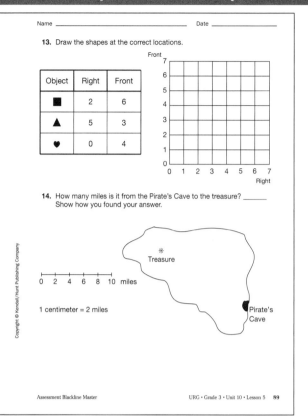

Unit Resource Guide - page 89

Unit Resource Guide (p. 90)

15. A. $2.50

B. $17.50

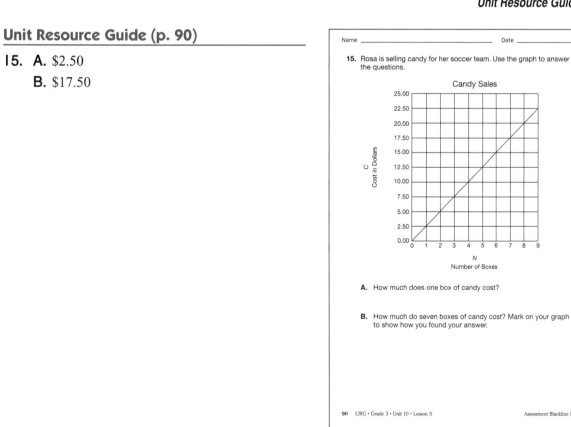

Unit Resource Guide - page 90

Discovery Assignment Book (p. 144)

Part 1

1. 8	2. 9
3. 90	4. 9
5. 8	6. 80
7. 7	8. 6
9. 50	10. 8
11. 7	12. 70
13. 50	14. 40
15. 70	

Part 2

1. 8853 (9876 − 1023)

2. 25. There are several ways to get this answer. One way is 4012 − 3987. There are many other combinations that give small differences (but not the smallest). For example, 2034 − 1987 = 47.

3. 9999 or 8999 (If leading 0 is allowed, 9999 − 0000 = 9999; if leading 0 is not allowed, 9999 − 1000 = 8999.)

4. 0 (If leading 0 is allowed, 0000 − 0000 = 0. If leading 0 is not allowed, 1000 − 1000 = 0.)

5. 667

6. 343

7. 111

8. Possible strategy: 1200 − 600 = 600.

Discovery Assignment Book (p. 145)

Part 3

1. A. six 8-gram masses, one 4-gram mass, and two 1-gram masses

   B. fifty-four 1-gram masses

2. A. seven 8-gram masses and two 1-gram masses

   B. Possible responses: three 8-gram masses and two 1-gram masses

Part 4

1. $7\frac{1}{2}$ hours

2. 30 hours

3. 11:30 A.M.

Discovery Assignment Book - page 144

Name _____ Date _____

Unit 10 Home Practice

PART 1

Do these problems in your head. Write only the answers.

1. 16 − 8 = _____   2. 17 − 8 = _____   3. 170 − 80 = _____
4. 18 − 9 = _____   5. 18 − 10 = _____   6. 150 − 70 = _____
7. 14 − 7 = _____   8. 14 − 8 = _____   9. 120 − 70 = _____
10. 14 − 6 = _____   11. 12 − 5 = _____   12. 120 − 50 = _____

13. 100
    − 50

14.   80
    − 40

15. 150
    − 80

PART 2

Put a digit (1, 2, 3, 4, 5, 6, 7, 8, 9, or 0) in each box. Use each digit once or not at all. Subtract to find your answers.

☐☐☐☐ − ☐☐☐☐ =

1. What is the biggest answer you can get? _____

2. What is the smallest answer you can get? _____

3. If a digit can be used more than once, then what is the biggest answer you can get? _____

4. If a digit can be used more than once, then what is the smallest answer you can get? _____

Solve the following problems. Estimate to be sure your answers are reasonable.

5.   1234
    − 567

6.   912
    − 569

7.   807
    − 696

8. Show your estimation strategy for Question 5.

144 DAB • Grade 3 • Unit 10   NUMBERS AND PATTERNS: AN ASSESSMENT UNIT

Discovery Assignment Book - page 144

Name _____ Date _____

PART 3

1. Suppose we use the following standard masses to measure mass using a balance: 8-gram masses, 4-gram masses, and 1-gram masses. Think about how many of each you would need to use to balance a bottle of glue with a mass of 54 grams.

   A. How many of each would you need if you used the smallest number of masses possible?

   _____

   B. How many of each would you need if you used the largest number of masses possible?

   _____

2. Using the same standard masses, think about how many of each you would need to balance a note pad with a mass of 58 grams.

   A. How many of each would you need if you used the smallest number of masses possible?

   _____

   B. If you started with eight 4-gram masses, how many 8-gram and 1-gram masses would you still need to balance the note pad?

   _____

PART 4

1. Mr. Sosa teaches art class from 8:00 A.M. until 3:30 P.M. every Saturday. How many hours does he work on one Saturday?

   _____

2. How many hours will Mr. Sosa have worked after 4 Saturdays?

   _____

3. Last Saturday Mr. Sosa started art class at 8:00 A.M. He got sick and ended class $3\frac{1}{2}$ hours later. What time did he end the class?

   _____

NUMBERS AND PATTERNS: AN ASSESSMENT UNIT   DAB • Grade 3 • Unit 10 **145**

Discovery Assignment Book - page 145

Glossary

This glossary provides definitions of key vocabulary terms in the Grade 3 lessons. Locations of key vocabulary terms in the curriculum are included with each definition. Components Key: URG = *Unit Resource Guide,* SG = *Student Guide,* and DAB = *Discovery Assignment Book.*

A

Area (URG Unit 5; SG Unit 5)
The area of a shape is the amount of space it covers, measured in square units.

Array (URG Unit 7 & Unit 11)
An array is an arrangement of elements into a rectangular pattern of (horizontal) rows and (vertical) columns. (*See* column and row.)

Associative Property of Addition (URG Unit 2)
For any three numbers a, b, and c we have $a + (b + c) = (a + b) + c$. For example in finding the sum of 4, 8, and 2, one can compute $4 + 8$ first and then add 2: $(4 + 8) + 2 = 14$. Alternatively, we can compute $8 + 2$ and then add the result to 4: $4 + (8 + 2) = 4 + 10 = 14$.

Average (URG Unit 5)
A number that can be used to represent a typical value in a set of data. (*See also* mean and median.)

Axes (URG Unit 8; SG Unit 8)
Reference lines on a graph. In the Cartesian coordinate system, the axes are two perpendicular lines that meet at the origin. The singular of axes is axis.

B

Base (of a cube model) (URG Unit 18; SG Unit 18)
The part of a cube model that sits on the "ground."

Base-Ten Board (URG Unit 4)
A tool to help children organize base-ten pieces when they are representing numbers.

Base-Ten Pieces (URG Unit 4; SG Unit 4)
A set of manipulatives used to model our number system as shown in the figure at the right. Note that a skinny is made of 10 bits, a flat is made of 100 bits, and a pack is made of 1000 bits.

Base-Ten Shorthand (SG Unit 4)
A pictorial representation of the base-ten pieces as shown.

Nickname	Picture	Shorthand
bit		·
skinny		/
flat		
pack		

Best-Fit Line (URG Unit 9; SG Unit 9; DAB Unit 9)
The line that comes closest to the most number of points on a point graph.

Bit (URG Unit 4; SG Unit 4)
A cube that measures 1 cm on each edge. It is the smallest of the base-ten pieces that is often used to represent 1. (*See also* base-ten pieces.)

C

Capacity (URG Unit 16)
1. The volume of the inside of a container.
2. The largest volume a container can hold.

Cartesian Coordinate System (URG Unit 8)
A method of locating points on a flat surface by means of numbers. This method is named after its originator, René Descartes. (*See also* coordinates.)

Centimeter (cm)
A unit of measure in the metric system equal to one-hundredth of a meter. (1 inch = 2.54 cm)

Column (URG Unit 11)
In an array, the objects lined up vertically.

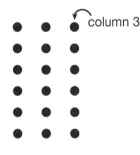
column 3

Common Fraction (URG Unit 15)
Any fraction that is written with a numerator and denominator that are whole numbers. For example, $\frac{3}{4}$ and $\frac{9}{4}$ are both common fractions. (*See also* decimal fraction.)

Commutative Property of Addition (URG Unit 2 & Unit 11)
This is also known as the Order Property of Addition. Changing the order of the addends does not change the sum. For example, $3 + 5 = 5 + 3 = 8$. Using variables, $n + m = m + n$.

Commutative Property of Multiplication (URG Unit 11)
Changing the order of the factors in a multiplication problem does not change the result, e.g., $7 \times 3 = 3 \times 7 = 21$. (*See also* turn-around facts.)

Congruent (URG Unit 12 & Unit 17; SG Unit 12)
Figures with the same shape and size.

Convenient Number (URG Unit 6)
A number used in computation that is close enough to give a good estimate, but is also easy to compute mentally, e.g., 25 and 30 are convenient numbers for 27.

Coordinates (URG Unit 8; SG Unit 8)
An ordered pair of numbers that locates points on a flat surface by giving distances from a pair of coordinate axes. For example, if a point has coordinates (4, 5) it is 4 units from the vertical axis and 5 units from the horizontal axis.

Counting Back (URG Unit 2)
A strategy for subtracting in which students start from a larger number and then count down until the number is reached. For example, to solve $8 - 3$, begin with 8 and count down three, 7, 6, 5.

Counting Down (*See* counting back.)

Counting Up (URG Unit 2)
A strategy for subtraction in which the student starts at the lower number and counts on to the higher number. For example, to solve $8 - 5$, the student starts at 5 and counts up three numbers (6, 7, 8). So $8 - 5 = 3$.

Cube (SG Unit 18)
A three-dimensional shape with six congruent square faces.

Cubic Centimeter (cc) (URG Unit 16; SG Unit 16)
The volume of a cube that is one centimeter long on each edge.

1 cm
1 cm
1 cm
cubic centimeter

Cup (URG Unit 16)
A unit of volume equal to 8 fluid ounces, one-half pint.

D

Decimal Fraction (URG Unit 15)
A fraction written as a decimal. For example, 0.75 and 0.4 are decimal fractions and $\frac{75}{100}$ and $\frac{4}{10}$ are called common fractions. (*See also* fraction.)

Denominator (URG Unit 13)
The number below the line in a fraction. The denominator indicates the number of equal parts in which the unit whole is divided. For example, the 5 is the denominator in the fraction $\frac{2}{5}$. In this case the unit whole is divided into five equal parts.

Density (URG Unit 16)
The ratio of an object's mass to its volume.

Difference (URG Unit 2)
The answer to a subtraction problem.

Dissection (URG Unit 12 & Unit 17)
Cutting or decomposing a geometric shape into smaller shapes that cover it exactly.

Distributive Property of Multiplication over Addition (URG Unit 19)
For any three numbers *a, b,* and *c, $a \times (b + c) = a \times b + a \times c$.* The distributive property is the foundation for most methods of multidigit multiplication. For example, $9 \times (17) = 9 \times (10 + 7) = 9 \times 10 + 9 \times 7 = 90 + 63 = 153$.

E

Equal-Arm Balance
See two-pan balance.

Equilateral Triangle (URG Unit 7)
A triangle with all sides of equal length and all angles of equal measure.

Equivalent Fractions (SG Unit 17)
Fractions that have the same value, e.g., $\frac{2}{4} = \frac{1}{2}$.

Estimate (URG Unit 5 & Unit 6)
1. (verb) To find *about* how many.
2. (noun) An approximate number.

Extrapolation (URG Unit 7)
Using patterns in data to make predictions or to estimate values that lie beyond the range of values in the set of data.

F

Fact Family (URG Unit 11; SG Unit 11)
Related math facts, e.g., $3 \times 4 = 12$, $4 \times 3 = 12$, $12 \div 3 = 4$, $12 \div 4 = 3$.

Factor (URG Unit 11; SG Unit 11)
1. In a multiplication problem, the numbers that are multiplied together. In the problem $3 \times 4 = 12$, 3 and 4 are the factors.
2. Whole numbers that can be multiplied together to get a number. That is, numbers that divide a number evenly, e.g., 1, 2, 3, 4, 6, and 12 are all the factors of 12.

Fewest Pieces Rule (URG Unit 4 & Unit 6; SG Unit 4)
Using the least number of base-ten pieces to represent a number. (*See also* base-ten pieces.)

Flat (URG Unit 4; SG Unit 4)
A block that measures 1 cm $\times$ 10 cm $\times$ 10 cm. It is one of the base-ten pieces that is often used to represent 100. (*See also* base-ten pieces.)

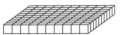

Flip (URG Unit 12)
A motion of the plane in which a figure is reflected over a line so that any point and its image are the same distance from the line.

Fraction (URG Unit 15)
A number that can be written as $\frac{a}{b}$ where a and b are whole numbers and b is not zero. For example, $\frac{1}{2}$, 0.5, and 2 are all fractions since 0.5 can be written as $\frac{5}{10}$ and 2 can be written as $\frac{2}{1}$.

Front-End Estimation (URG Unit 6)
Estimation by looking at the left-most digit.

G

Gallon (gal) (URG Unit 16)
A unit of volume equal to four quarts.

Gram
The basic unit used to measure mass.

H

Hexagon (SG Unit 12)
A six-sided polygon.

Horizontal Axis (SG Unit 1)
In a coordinate grid, the *x*-axis. The axis that extends from left to right.

I

Interpolation (URG Unit 7)
Making predictions or estimating values that lie between data points in a set of data.

J

K

Kilogram
1000 grams.

L

Likely Event (SG Unit 1)
An event that has a high probability of occurring.

Line of Symmetry (URG Unit 12)
A line is a line of symmetry for a plane figure if, when the figure is folded along this line, the two parts match exactly.

Line Symmetry (URG Unit 12; SG Unit 12)
A figure has line symmetry if it has at least one line of symmetry.

Liter (l) (URG Unit 16; SG Unit 16)
Metric unit used to measure volume. A liter is a little more than a quart.

M

Magic Square (URG Unit 2)
A square array of digits in which the sums of the rows, columns, and main diagonals are the same.

Making a Ten (URG Unit 2)
Strategies for addition and subtraction that make use of knowing the sums to ten. For example, knowing $6 + 4 = 10$ can be helpful in finding $10 - 6 = 4$ and $11 - 6 = 5$.

Mass (URG Unit 9 & Unit 16; SG Unit 9)
The amount of matter in an object.

Mean (URG Unit 5)
An average of a set of numbers that is found by adding the values of the data and dividing by the number of values.

Measurement Division (URG Unit 7)
Division as equal grouping. The total number of objects and the number of objects in each group are known. The number of groups is the unknown. For example, tulip bulbs come in packages of 8. If 216 bulbs are sold, how many packages are sold?

Measurement Error (URG Unit 9)
The unavoidable error that occurs due to the limitations inherent to any measurement instrument.

Median (URG Unit 5; DAB Unit 5)
For a set with an odd number of data arranged in order, it is the middle number. For an even number of data arranged in order, it is the number halfway between the two middle numbers.

Meniscus (URG Unit 16; SG Unit 16)
The curved surface formed when a liquid creeps up the side of a container (for example, a graduated cylinder).

Meter (m)
The standard unit of length measure in the metric system. One meter is approximately 39 inches.

Milliliter (ml) (URG Unit 16; SG Unit 16)
A measure of capacity in the metric system that is the volume of a cube that is one centimeter long on each edge.

Multiple (URG Unit 3 & Unit 11)
A number is a multiple of another number if it is evenly divisible by that number. For example, 12 is a multiple of 2 since 2 divides 12 evenly.

N

Numerator (URG Unit 13)
The number written above the line in a fraction. For example, the 2 is the numerator in the fraction $\frac{2}{5}$. (*See also* denominator.)

O

One-Dimensional Object (URG Unit 18; SG Unit 18)
An object is one-dimensional if it is made up of pieces of lines and curves.

Ordered Pairs (URG Unit 8)
A pair of numbers that gives the coordinates of a point on a grid in relation to the origin. The horizontal coordinate is given first; the vertical coordinate is given second. For example, the ordered pair (5, 3) tells us to move five units to the right of the origin and 3 units up.

Origin (URG Unit 8)
The point at which the *x*- and *y*-axes (horizontal and vertical axes) intersect on a coordinate plane. The origin is described by the ordered pair (0, 0) and serves as a reference point so that all the points on the plane can be located by ordered pairs.

P

Pack (URG Unit 4; SG Unit 4)
A cube that measures 10 cm on each edge. It is one of the base-ten pieces that is often used to represent 1000. (*See also* base-ten pieces.)

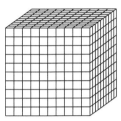

Palindrome (URG Unit 6)
A number, word, or phrase that reads the same forward and backward, e.g., 12321.

Parallel Lines (URG Unit 18)
Lines that are in the same direction. In the plane, parallel lines are lines that do not intersect.

Parallelogram (URG Unit 18)
A quadrilateral with two pairs of parallel sides.

Partitive Division (URG Unit 7)
Division as equal sharing. The total number of objects and the number of groups are known. The number of objects in each group is the unknown. For example, Frank has 144 marbles that he divides equally into 6 groups. How many marbles are in each group?

Pentagon (SG Unit 12)
A five-sided, five-angled polygon.

Perimeter (URG Unit 7; DAB Unit 7)
The distance around a two-dimensional shape.

Pint (URG Unit 16)
A unit of volume measure equal to 16 fluid ounces, i.e., two cups.

Polygon
A two-dimensional connected figure made of line segments in which each endpoint of every side meets with an endpoint of exactly one other side.

Population (URG Unit 1; SG Unit 1)
A collection of persons or things whose properties will be analyzed in a survey or experiment.

Prediction (SG Unit 1)
Using data to declare or foretell what is likely to occur.

Prime Number (URG Unit 11)
A number that has exactly two factors. For example, 7 has exactly two distinct factors, 1 and 7.

Prism
A three-dimensional figure that has two congruent faces, called bases, that are parallel to each other, and all other faces are parallelograms.

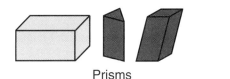
Prisms

Not a prism

Product (URG Unit 11; SG Unit 11; DAB Unit 11)
The answer to a multiplication problem. In the problem $3 \times 4 = 12$, 12 is the product.

Q

Quadrilateral (URG Unit 18)
A polygon with four sides.

Quart (URG Unit 16)
A unit of volume equal to 32 fluid ounces; one quarter of a gallon.

R

Recording Sheet (URG Unit 4)
A place value chart used for addition and subtraction problems.

Rectangular Prism (URG Unit 18; SG Unit 18)
A prism whose bases are rectangles. A right rectangular prism is a prism having all faces rectangles.

Regular (URG Unit 7; DAB Unit 7)
A polygon is regular if all sides are of equal length and all angles are equal.

Remainder (URG Unit 7)
Something that remains or is left after a division problem. The portion of the dividend that is not evenly divisible by the divisor, e.g., $16 \div 5 = 3$ with 1 as a remainder.

Right Angle (SG Unit 12)
An angle that measures $90°$.

Rotation (turn) (URG Unit 12)
A transformation (motion) in which a figure is turned a specified angle and direction around a point.

Row (URG Unit 11)
In an array, the objects lined up horizontally.

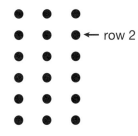
← row 2

Rubric (URG Unit 2)
A written guideline for assigning scores to student work, for the purpose of assessment.

S

Sample (URG Unit 1; SG Unit 1)
A part or subset of a population.

Skinny (URG Unit 4; SG Unit 4)
A block that measures 1 cm $\times$ 1 cm $\times$ 10 cm. It is one of the base-ten pieces that is often used to represent 10. (*See also* base-ten pieces.)

Square Centimeter (sq cm) (SG Unit 5)
The area of a square that is 1 cm long on each side.

Square Number (SG Unit 11)
A number that is the product of a whole number multiplied by itself. For example, 25 is a square number since $5 \times 5 = 25$. A square number can be represented by a square array with the same number of rows as columns. A square array for 25 has 5 rows of 5 objects in each row or 25 total objects.

Standard Masses
A set of objects with convenient masses, usually 1 g, 10 g, 100 g, etc.

Sum (URG Unit 2; SG Unit 2)
The answer to an addition problem.

Survey (URG Unit 14; SG Unit 14)
An investigation conducted by collecting data from a sample of a population and then analyzing it. Usually surveys are used to make predictions about the entire population.

T

Tangrams (SG Unit 12)
A type of geometric puzzle. A shape is given and it must be covered exactly with seven standard shapes called tans.

Thinking Addition (URG Unit 2)
A strategy for subtraction that uses a related addition problem. For example, $15 - 7 = 8$ because $8 + 7 = 15$.

Three-Dimensional (URG Unit 18; SG Unit 18)
Existing in three-dimensional space; having length, width, and depth.

TIMS Laboratory Method (URG Unit 1; SG Unit 1)
A method that students use to organize experiments and investigations. It involves four components: draw, collect, graph, and explore. It is a way to help students learn about the scientific method.

Turn (URG Unit 12)
(*See* rotation.)

Turn-Around Facts (URG Unit 2 & Unit 11 p. 37; SG Unit 11)
Addition facts that have the same addends but in a different order, e.g., $3 + 4 = 7$ and $4 + 3 = 7$. (*See also* commutative property of addition and commutative property of multiplication.)

Two-Dimensional (URG Unit 18; SG Unit 18)
Existing in the plane; having length and width.

Two-Pan Balance
A device for measuring the mass of an object by balancing the object against a number of standard masses (usually multiples of 1 unit, 10 units, and 100 units, etc.).

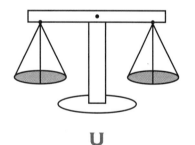

U

Unit (of measurement) (URG Unit 18)
A precisely fixed quantity used to measure. For example, centimeter, foot, kilogram, and quart are units of measurement.

Using a Ten (URG Unit 2)
1. A strategy for addition that uses partitions of the number 10. For example, one can find $8 + 6$ by thinking $8 + 6 = 8 + 2 + 4 = 10 + 4 = 14$.
2. A strategy for subtraction that uses facts that involve subtracting 10. For example, students can use $17 - 10 = 7$ to learn the "close fact" $17 - 9 = 8$.

Using Doubles (URG Unit 2)
Strategies for addition and subtraction that use knowing doubles. For example, one can find $7 + 8$ by thinking $7 + 8 = 7 + 7 + 1 = 14 + 1 = 15$. Knowing $7 + 7 = 14$ can be helpful in finding $14 - 7 = 7$ and $14 - 8 = 6$.

V

Value (URG Unit 1; SG Unit 1)
The possible outcomes of a variable. For example, red, green, and blue are possible values for the variable *color.* Two meters and 1.65 meters are possible values for the variable *length.*

Variable (URG Unit 1; SG Unit 1)
1. An attribute or quantity that changes or varies.
2. A symbol that can stand for a variable.

Vertex (URG Unit 12; SG Unit 12)
1. A point where the sides of a polygon meet.
2. A point where the edges of a three-dimensional object meet.

Vertical Axis (SG Unit 1)
In a coordinate grid, the y-axis. It is perpendicular to the horizontal axis.

Volume (URG Unit 16; SG Unit 16)
The measure of the amount of space occupied by an object.

Volume by Displacement (URG Unit 16)
A way of measuring volume of an object by measuring the amount of water (or some other fluid) it displaces.

W

Weight (URG Unit 9)
A measure of the pull of gravity on an object. One unit for measuring weight is the pound.

X

Y

Z